New Directions
in Russian
International Studies

Edited by
Andrei P. Tsygankov and Pavel A. Tsygankov

Andrei P. Tsygankov and Pavel A. Tsygankov (Eds.)

NEW DIRECTIONS IN RUSSIAN INTERNATIONAL STUDIES

ibidem-Verlag
Stuttgart

Bibliografische Information Der Deutschen Bibliothek

Die Deutsche Bibliothek verzeichnet diese Publikation in der Deutschen Nationalbibliografie; detaillierte bibliografische Daten sind im Internet über <http://dnb.ddb.de> abrufbar.

∞

Gedruckt auf alterungsbeständigem, säurefreien Papier
Printed on acid-free paper

ISSN: 1614-3515

ISBN: 3-89821-422-2

© *ibidem*-Verlag
Stuttgart 2005
Alle Rechte vorbehalten

Printed in Germany

Contents

Acknowledgements

This collection of essay has been originally published as a special issue of *Communist and Post-Communist Studies*, Vol. 37, No. 1, March 2004. We wish to thank the journal editors Andrzej Korbonski, Lucy Kerner, and Luba Fajfer for their permission to re-publish the essays in this volume. This project would have not been possible without support from Dean Joel Kassiola and the College of Behavioral and Social Science at San Francisco State University. We gratefully acknowledge this support. For helpful comments and editorial suggestions, we are especially grateful to Andrzej Korbonski, Lucy Kerner, and Andreas Umland. Furthermore, we would like to thank Natalya Valentova and Anna Radivilova for their assistance with translating and editing manuscripts for this issue. Finally, we are grateful to Julia V. Godzikovskaya for assisting in preparing the manucript for publication. The authors alone are responsible for the remaining errors.

Abstracts

New directions in Russian international studies: pluralization, Westernization, and isolationism

Andrei P. Tsygankov and Pavel A. Tsygankov

The essay argues that Western scholars can improve their understanding of post-Soviet Russia by studying the new discipline of new Russian International Relations (IR). The other objective of the essay is to move away from the excessively West-centered IR scholarship by exploring indigenous Russian perceptions and inviting a dialogue across the globe. The essay identifies key trends in Russian IR knowledge reflective of the transitional nature of Russia's post-Soviet change. It argues that Russian IR continues to be in a stage of ideological and theoretical uncertainty, which is a result of unresolved questions of national identity. For describing Russia's identity crisis, the authors employ Erving Goffman's concept of *stigma* defined as a crisis of social acceptance by Russia's significant Other (West). The essay suggests that, until this crisis is resolved, much of Russian IR debates can be understood in terms of search for a national idea. It also introduces the authors of the volume and summarizes their contribution to our understanding of Russian (and Western) IR.

Discussions of international relations in post-communist Russia

Alexandr A. Sergunin

The article describes the progress in Russian theoretical thinking about the world. The author reviews post-Soviet IR discussions and traces how they progressed from one paradigm to another in response to shifts in social issues and political agendas. The paper concludes that although realism has emerged as a prominent theoretical paradigm, Russian IR is still in a process of its self-definition and remains widely open to various intellectual influences.

The Russian Realist school of international relations

Tatyana A. Shakleyina and Alexei D. Bogaturov

This article analyses the realist school in Russian International Relations scholarship and introduces the debates among Russian realists. It focuses on the characteristics of the newly-emerging world order and the development of an adequate strategy for Russia to pursue in its international undertakings. The authors argue that, over the 1990s, realism has made considerable intellectual progress and has gained the status of a leading intellectual movement in Russia. It assisted the Russian intellectual and political community in defining the country's interests and priorities in the emerging international relations, and it provided a necessary analysis of the world order's structure and polarity.

Dilemmas and promises of Russian liberalism

Pavel A. Tsygankov and Andrei P. Tsygankov

The authors analyze the divisions within Russian liberalism—another influential IR theory—and the contradictory nature of this intellectual movement. In particular, they draw attention to the debate between pro-Western and more nationally-oriented liberals, which they propose to understand in terms of the familiar disagreement between supporters of cosmopolitan and communitarian thought. Whereas cosmopolitans insist on the emergence of a single humanity and emphasize factors of a unifying and homogenizing nature, communitarians underscore the role of national and cultural bases for building democratic institutions in the world. The authors trace how various liberal currents understand the nature of the post-Cold War order, Russia's national interests, and its foreign policy orientations.

Studies of globalization and equity in post-Soviet Russia

Mikhail V. Il'yin

The article reports on the progress of Russian research on globalization and equity. Building on Stein Rokkan's classification of social cleavages, the author identifies several schools in Russian globalization studies. Namely, he discusses how the distinctions of *authority—people, church—state, land—indus-*

try, owners—workers, metropolis—colony, and *network—hierarchy* find their reflection in current Russian research. The article shows that Russian scholars have recently engaged in a series of discussions of globalization's equity criteria and democratic governance applying the world system approaches, civilization analysis, and the theory of Kondratieff's cycles.

Geopolitics in Russia—science or vocation?
Eduard G. Solovyev

The author describes the development of geopolitical studies in Russia after the Soviet breakup. He identifies two main schools of geopolitical analysis, Traditionalism and Revisionism. Traditionalism is inspired by old European and Russian geopolitical theories and views the world through the lens of confrontation over power and resources. The revisionist school, on the other hand, adopts a considerably broader definition of what constitutes geopolitics by proposing to study various forms of organizing space on a global scale. According to the paper's central argument, Russian geopolitics, while having emerged as a vocation, it is yet to turn into a fully-fledged academic discipline. It continues to lack coherent and scientifically testable theoretical propositions and needs a broad discussion of its issues with the participation of both traditionalists and revisionists.

Ethnicity and the study of international relations in post-Soviet Russia
Nayil' M. Mukharyamov

The essay concentrates on Russian studies of ethnicity and identifies Substantialist and Relational approaches to studying ethnicity in international relations. Substantialists see the impact of ethnicity as the main organizing force of international politics and posit states as principally ethnocentric units driven by ambitions of large ethnic groups. In their turn, Relationists question the essentialist assumptions and seek to depoliticize the notion of ethnicity. Rather than concentrating on states or large ethnic groups in international politics, they take the individual as the main unit of analysis and argue that ethnicity is a choice, not destiny. The author sees both substantialism and relationism as actively developing in Russia and associates progress in the field with further development and cross-fertilization of the two ideas.

The study of international political economy
Stanislav L. Tkachenko

The author argues that International Political Economy (IPE), however prominent in the West, is not nearly as established in Russia as an academic discipline. In the Russian policy community, the main debate is between Liberal Institutionalists, who advocate the country's integration into the global economy, and the so-called Dirigists, who promote relative economic autonomy. These two schools' ideas, however, only begin to find their way into academia. Three main problems impede IPE development in Russian academia — a strict separation of political science from economics, a deficit of theoretical generalization, and weaknesses of the of educational curriculum.

From prominence to decline:
Russian studies of international negotiations
Marina M. Lebedeva

The essay analyzes progress in the field of international negotiations. In the author's assessment, Russian research on negotiations, once a prominent discipline, is currently in decline. Despite the persistent need to study international negotiations, most scholars that had formerly been active in the field have moved to other areas. The rise of new issues demanding urgent attention, the principally changed shape of international negotiations' *problematique*, as well as serious financial difficulties have all contributed to the discipline's decline. The author ends on a positive note and expresses the conviction that international negotiations will be revived as an academic field in Russia. She bases that conviction on the country's practical needs, as well as its growing integration into Western IR studies.

I. New directions in Russian international studies: pluralization, Westernization, and isolationism

Andrei P. Tsygankov and Pavel A. Tsygankov

1. Introduction

Russian society has changed dramatically after the USSR's disintegration. By no stretch of imagination can the post-Soviet society be described as "totalitarian," "communist," or "autoritarian." In attempting to understand the social and political system that has emerged after the USSR, scholars have produced a plethora of new conceptual labels and theories, such as "electoral monarchy," "market bolshevism," or "illiberal democracy" (Klyamkin and Shevtsova 1999; Reddaway and Glinski 2001; Sakwa 2002, 455). Yet there has been little systematic effort to understand the paths of academic knowledge emerging as a foundation of new Russian society. In order to contribute to filling this gap, we have selected for analysis one branch of Russian newly emerging Social Science—International Relations.[1]

The new Russian IR has been understudied. Aside from rare individual articles,[2] there has been practically no effort to investigate the subject in the West.[3] The contrast with the wealth of Western studies of the Soviet IR is a striking one.[4] Russia is no longer a threat to the West, and that alone seems to have directed some of the sharpest pens away from studying this country's

---

[1] We hope that others attempt similar analyses of the state of Russia's other Social Sciences—Sociology, Sociolinguistics, Political Science, and Modern History. For a recent cross-disciplinary analysis of postcommunist transformation, see Bonker, Muller, and Pickel 2002.

[2] Kubalkova 1992; Patomaki in Millennium 1999; Sergunin 2000; Andrei Tsygankov 2003a, 2004.

[3] Russians, on the other hand, study Western IR very carefully. For recent reviews of Western IR theories by Russian academics, see especially Pavel Tsygankov 1998, 2002; Lebedeva 2003.

[4] For studies of Soviet IR, see especially, Zimmerman 1967; Kubalkova and Cruickshank 1985; Hough 1986, Lynch 1987; Shenfield 1987; Light 1988.

attitudes and behavior. Yet the non-threatening Russia is not a less interesting one, and Western scholars have not come to understand Russia better just because the Iron Curtain is no longer in place.

Analyzing the emerging Russian IR can help us answer some of the key questions about Russia. How does the new Russia see itself in the world? How does it perceive the new international environment? Which social and political institutions does it see appropriate to develop after the end of the Cold War? These are the questions that are at the heart of the new Russian IR scholarship, and these are the questions that continue to drive Western scholarship about the new Russia. The central question behind our IR story is also the question of the new Russian society. By tracing the processes of knowledge accumulation in Russian IR, we hope to contribute to the understanding of how much and in which direction this society has changed since 1991.

Our second goal is more specific: it is the development of international studies as a global discipline. For a long time, International Relations has been developing as an excessively West-centric and pro-Western branch of research. As many scholars pointed out, IR all too often reflects political, ideological, and epistemological biases of Western, particularly American, civilization.[5] As a result, a perception has developed across the world that Western IR—and Western Social Science in general—is nothing but a sophisticated ideology and a set of conceptual tools that serve to justify Western global hegemony. In various parts of the globe, West-centered world-order projects have often been perceived as unable to promote a just and stable international system because of their exclusively Western orientations and lack of empathetic understanding of other cultures. Some scholars have argued that rather than promoting the dialogue necessary for finding an appropriate international system, these projects contribute to further isolationism and hostility among international actors (Alker et al. 1998; Rajaee 2000; Tsygankov, 2004). We

---

[5] For various analyses of International Relations as a discipline that is ethnocentric and reflects American/Western civilizational biases, see Hoffmann 1977; Alker and Biersteker 1983; Holsti 1985; Inayatullah and Blaney 1996; Waever 1998; Crawford and Jarvis 2001. The ethnocentrism, of course, may be just as widespread in non-Western cultural contexts—Russian, Chinese, Iranian, and other—an issue that still awaits its researchers.

would like to challenge the perception that IR is primarily about justifying the West's cultural hegemony and to move away from the identified ethnocentrism of IR knowledge. Taking Russian IR seriously is a step in this direction. By exploring indigenous analytical impulses and perceptions, we hope to move away from excessively West-centered IR scholarship, invite a dialogue across the globe and therefore enrich our knowledge about the world.

In this essay, we identify pluralization, Westernization, and isolation as key trends in Russian IR knowledge cumulation. These trends do not yet reflect the emergence of some cohesive paradigm of knowledge and are reflective of the transitional nature of Russia's post-Soviet change. Unlike the United States, Great Britain, or China, Russia has not yet developed its own ideological "mainstream" in international studies. While the "great" ideas of "democratic peace," "international society," and "great harmony," respectively, serve to provide such a mainstream in the three identified countries (Callahan 2003), Russia remains a playground of ideological and theoretical competition. Examples of such ideological competition include those of the Eurasianists versus Westernizers, Democrats versus supporters of the Strong State, and Ethnonationalists versus Civic Identity advocates.[6]

Russia therefore has decided against Soviet Marxism,[7] but not yet in favor of the next "great" post-Soviet idea. *Pluralization* of Russian IR has emerged in response to the decline of Soviet Marxism, and it signifies a growing diversity of social science in the absence of a framework for growth of academic knowledge. In the absence of such a framework, current Russian IR can be described in terms of contestation between two additional key trends—Westernization and isolationism—that have emerged as a response to the identified

---

[6]   The articles collected in this issue by Sergunin, Shakleyina and Bogaturov, Solovyev, and Mukharyamov analyze these ideological and theoretical discussions in greater detail.

[7]   By "Soviet Marxism," we understand the Soviet Leninist-Stalinist interpretation of Marx's original work. Although Soviet Marxism was in many respects principally different from what Marx had intended, its commitments to eradicating private property, religion, and other "bourgeois" institutions from social life allow us to place Soviet Marxism within the broader Marxist tradition. The term "Soviet Marxism" is not new and has been used before by both leftist (Marcuse 1958) and conservative thinkers (Kolakowski 1978). We further elaborate on our understanding of the term below.

ideological and theoretical vacuum. While *Westernization* implies Russia's growing dependence on the West's mainstream theoretical concepts and its mode of knowledge cumulation, *Isolationism* is recessive and represents an essentialist reaction to the excesses of Western positivism. While the trend of Westernization helps to bring Russian IR in tune with social science developments in the West, it also holds the potential of underestimating the indigenous intellectual tradition. Isolationism responds to the excesses of Westernization and calls for Russia's autarchic intellectual development, thereby depriving Russian IR of opportunities to learn from foreign cultures and social sciences. Both of these trends are influential in current Russian international studies. The essays in this issue further describe and, to some degree, represent the identified trends of pluralization, Westernization, and isolation in the country's relatively new discipline.

This ideological and theoretical uncertainty of Russian IR can be understood as a result of unresolved questions of Russia's national identity. Until Russia knows what it is and until it clearly defines its post-Soviet values and international orientations, Russian IR will remain an area of ideological contestation. The roots of Russia's identity crisis can be understood with the help of Erving Goffman's (1963) concept of *stigma*, which he defined as a crisis of broader social acceptance. The fact that for almost the entire twentieth century Russia has been "disqualified from full social acceptance" (Goffman 1963, i) by its "significant other" (West) contributed greatly to the country's current identity crisis, in which the choice of a "great" idea is yet to be made. The West has yet to accept Russia as a part of itself, and Russian society has yet to develop its identification with the West.[8] So long as this is the case, much of Russian IR debates should be understood in terms of the country's search for a "great" idea.[9]

---

[8] Some data strongly indicates that the Russian public is well aware of the society's cultural distinctivness from the West. In December 2001, according to the respected polling agency VTSIOM, 71 percent of Russians agreed with the statement that "Russia belongs to a special 'Eurasian' or Orthodox civilization, and therefore cannot follow the Western path of development." Only 13 percent counted Russia as a part of Western civilization (VTSIOM 2001).

The essay is organized as follows. The next section develops the notion of stigma in Russia's Soviet development. The sections 3 and 4 trace patterns of knowledge accumulation in new Russian IR. The final two sections introduce the authors of this issue and discuss their contribution to our understanding of Russian international studies. They also formulate conclusions about the over-all growth in Russian IR knowledge and its implications for future develop-ments in Russian and Western social sciences.

2. Soviet Marxism and the stigma of the Russian self

Russia's current identity crisis can be traced back to the developments before the Bolshevik revolution of October 1917. At the time, Europe played the role of Russia's significant Other, and, at least since Czar Peter the Great, had fig-ured prominently in Russia's debates on national identity. It was Europe that created the larger meaningful environment in which Russia's rulers defended their core values.[10] It was in the European context of secularization that Peter assumed power in 1694 and introduced a new ideology of state patriotism, or loyalty to the state (Tolz 2001, 27). However, the egalitarian ideas of the French revolution of 1789 split Europe into progressive and anti-revolutionary camps, and Russia had to decide between the two. Some rulers—most prominently Alexandr I and Alexandr II—attempted to yet again redefine the country's identity in line with the new European ideas of Enlightenment, Constitutionalism, and Capitalism. Others sought to defend the old Europe and preserve the basic features of the autocratic regime.

The Bolshevik revolution of October 1917 reflected the struggle of the two Europes and the resulting crisis of Russia's external identification. The spread of extremist Marxist ideas in Russia and the country's eventual break with Europe was a product of two factors: Europe's own agonizing identity crisis and Russia's rulers' unpreparedness to deal with the crisis. In the absence of the czar's ability to answer the newly emerged identity questions, it was the

---

[9]   We build here on some recent IR research that has further challenged the positivist con-cept of knowledge cumulation by emphasizing instead the national-cultural foundations of social science development (Weiver 1998; Callahan 2003).

[10]   On Russia's engagement with various European ideas, see especially Neumann 1996.

Bolsheviks who made the key identity choice by proclaiming Russia's break with its "bourgeois" past and in 1922 pronouncing it the Soviet Union. Unlike some previous critics of the two Europes, the Bolsheviks adopted not merely a *non*-European, but an *anti*-European identity.[11] Their socialist identity vision implied the perceived superiority of Russia relative to the liberal and autocratic Europes.

In this context, Soviet Marxism served as the new officially sanctioned "great" idea. It helped to legitimize Russia's new socialist identity and provided intellectuals with principally new lenses through which to analyze the world. Both onthologically and epistemologically, Marxism presented an important challenge to Western social sciences and International Relations. At least three key features deserve to be mentioned here. First, the new way of thinking about the world was *socially critical* or emancipatory. Marx's dictum that philosophers must go beyond explaining the world and toward changing it radically drew attention to the relationships between theory and practice and therefore shattered the very foundations of status-quo-oriented positivist thinking. Secondly, Marxist *historically-structural* approach meant to link world affairs to the existing phenomena of global exploitation and inequality and to reveal their origins and social roots. Finally, Marxist analysis was *holistic and global*, as it understood the world as globally united and globally divided at the same time. As opposed to the three familiar levels of analysis in mainstream International Relations—individual, national, and systemic—Marxism viewed the struggle for human liberation and emancipation as universal and without boundaries. All these features were instrumental in the subsequent development of critical tradition in international relations, both in the Soviet Russia and outside.[12]

---

[11] In response to the crisis of European identity, some Russian intellectuals began advocating a break with both old-nationalist and new-liberal Europes as early as in the 1840s-1850s. Alexandr Herzen, for instance, grew disappointed with European conservative restorations and—long before the Bolsheviks—turned to socialism arguing for Russia's own, non-European way of "catching up" economically and socially. The Bolsheviks pushed this line of thinking to its extreme.

[12] The fact that the critical tradition in Western IR is alive and well (see, for example, the recently published volume on historical materialism and globalization by Rupert and Smith 2002) should in part be attributed to the richness of Marxist social thinking.

However, Marxism played a dual role in Russia's social science and International Relations. By legitimizing Russia's new identity, the Soviet regime also developed a self-serving vision of Marxism and legitimized the country's social stigma, or the lack of its "self's" acceptance by the European "other." In addition to some of its progressive and liberating elements, the Soviet version of Marxism served as an ideologically pretentious way to preserve a statist status quo and as a tool of suppressing dissent. The lack of acceptance by the outside world further developed this defensiveness of Soviet Marxism into a siege mentality, with dire consequences for the social sciences.

Dogmatism and isolationism, in particular, set in as essential features of Soviet social science. The official ideological hegemony of Soviet Marxism stiffened creative thought by imposing rigid cannons on scholars of International Relations and encouraging dogmatic interpretations of world affairs. Epistemologically, scholars had to write in the crude positivist tradition of "we are ahead of the world and therefore know the truth," suppressing the critical potential of original Marxist theory. Substantively, IR "scholarship" was all too often reduced to interpretations of official documents and speeches of the leaders to the Communist Party Congresses.[13] Isolationism was also a product of the country's social stigma. Soviet Marxism allowed for only a minimal dialogue with non-Marxist scholars. Even Marxist and neo-Marxist developments outside the Soviet Union, such as the Frankfurt School in Germany, were not welcome. Cross-fertilization with the outside world was therefore negligible and confined to very narrow circles of elite scholars with privileged access to information.[14]

---

[13] The 1983 verdict of the General Secretary Yuri Andropov "we don't know the society in which we live" highlighted best that scholars were no longer in the business of raising new and important questions; instead, they were repeating and interpreting official mantras.

[14] Only in Moscow's special libraries that were closed to the public, some scholars were able to obtain access to books critical of the official Soviet Marxism. In order to secure such access, they had to obtain permission of their employers and the Communist Party authorities.

3. Pluralizarion and the birth of the new "self"

Russia's new search for its identity did not emerge after the Soviet disintegration but can rather be traced to the post-Stalin's era. As European crisis and confrontation gave a way to the continent's relative consolidation after the Second World War, Soviet rulers increasingly began to identify with the new liberal-democratic Europe and the West in general. The intercourse with Western ideas grew stronger after Nikita Khrushchev's famous de-Stalinization speech at the XXth Communist Party congress, in which he pledged, among other things, to bring Soviet Russia closer to Europe.[15] Despite Khrushchev's removal from power, the impact of de-Stalinization proved to be irreversible—a considerable part of a new intellectual generation now referred to themselves as the "children of the XXth party congress" and worked within and outside the establishment to bring Soviet Russia closer to the West.[16] It was the post-Stalin era that saw, in particular, a growth of specialized institutions in which researchers carefully analyzed mainstream Western ideas, such as those generated by American IR scholars.[17] Ultimately, it was Europe's and the West's new identity consolidation that brought to power the new Soviet leader, Mikhail Gorbachev, who proclaimed a new era in relationships with the West.

IR developments that accompanied these changes can be described as a growing pluralization of knowledge. By pluralization we mean the theoretical divergences from the official line of thinking that were taking place within Soviet social science. Soviet Marxism had never been entirely homogeneous—ever since the death of its founder, Vladimir Lenin, in 1924, at least two schools competed for the status of official ideology and "loyal" interpretor of Leninist intellectual legacy. Radicals advocated forceful methods of industrialization, whereas moderates argued for a more gradual process of development and proceeded from the late-Lenin's notion of "co-existence" with the Western "capitalist world." This debate had been shut down by Stalin after his

---

[15] Khrushchev saw Russia as culturally close to Europe, and at one point he proposed the mutual disbandment of NATO and the Warsaw Pact accompanied by withdrawal of American military forces from the continent (Donaldson and Nogee 1998, 69).

[16] For analyses of this era, see especially Arbatov 1992 and English 2000, chaps. 2-3.

[17] For details, see sources listed in fn. 4.

break with Lenin's post-1921 philosophy of moderation in relations with the peasant class and the external world, and was only revived after Stalin's death. Soviet Social Science also began to slowly absorb the ideas from the West and *Samizdat,*[18] some of which were revisionist Marxist in nature, others liberal and anti-communist, and still others fiercely nationalistic and critical of the official ideology from the traditionalist conservative perspective. Often without citing the original sources, some of the most daring social scientists began to use Western and Samizdat ideas in public discourse in order to advocate change from the past.[19]

Soviet decline and Gorbachev's Perestroika accelerated the pluralization of knowledge. Reflecting Gorbachev's own evolution, official Marxism evolved along the lines of European Social Democracy (Herman 1996; English 2000). Opposition to it came from the neo-orthodox thinking advocated by the newly emerged Communist Party of the Russian Federation and its leader Gennadi Zyuganov. Zyuganov's "Marxism" is a merger of old Stalinist ideas, traditional geopolitics, and Russian imperial nationalism (Zyuganov 1997, 1998). Aside from Gorbachev and Zyuganov, Marxist scholars also developed an interest in world-system approaches, often associated, in the West, with the name of Immanuel Wallerstein. Both Gorbachev's New Thinking and world system analysis, as Mikhail Il'yin suggests in this volume, continue a long-standing tradition of Marxist "global thinking" and have roots in domestic interest in global issues as the environment, population dynamics, and the arms race.

Outside of the Marxist worldview, a variety of new schools has emerged and began to develop. Most of them are heavily influenced by the ideas developed in the West as transmitted by local representatives of various social sciences. Following the three familiar perspectives in Western IR, the new

---

[18] *Samizdat* refers to self-produced, self-published, and self-circulated ideas that became characteristic of the post-Stalin's era.

[19] For instance, Gorbachev's team had been influenced by Western ideas of growing interdependence in the world before they came to power. Gorbachev was exposed to similar thinking through Georgi Shakhnazarov, his future advisor. Shakhnazarov first met Gorbachev in the early 1980s, and they had an extended conversation about world order and Shakhnazarov's unorthodox viewed expressed in his book *"Gryadushchi miroporyadok"* (1972), which Gorbachev had read (For more details, see Shakhnazarov 2000, 277-282).

Russian IR have developed their own Liberal, Realist, and Post-Structuralist camps. The rich essay by Alexandr Sergunin sensitizes us to the applicability of these approaches to Russia's cultural background and points out their diversity and intellectual indiginization. Liberals pursue the ideas of globalization and democratic peace and are often economists and political scientists by training.[20] Russian Realism is emerging as a complex intellectual movement, in which historians, philosophers, sociologists, and economists develop their own schools and research agendas. Russia's leading scholars Tatyana Shakleyina and Alexei Bogaturov identify six different groups or schools that currently exist within the country's Realist movement. They argue that most of these schools are relatively new although some can be traced back to the Soviet developments of the 1970s. Finally, Russia is beginning to respond, albeit slowly, to the Western "post-structural turn," and philosophers and sociologists are increasingly taking a lead in the post-structural movement.[21]

How healthy is pluralization of knowledge for Russia and Russian IR? As tentative as our evaluation can be, it is a welcome development that presents a sharp and refreshing contrast to the mentioned dogmatism and isolationism within the official Soviet paradigm. Clearly, it is only in dialogue with outside ideas and through national discussion that Russia can find its new "self" and free itself of the social stigma. At the same time, pluralization may have a negative effect on the growth of social science knowledge. Kalevi Holsti (1985) once expressed the concern that intellectual movements outside the mainstream of Western IR erode the foundations of the discipline and obstruct its further development.[22] If this concern has any merit in the Western context of a well-established tradition of IR theory, then it is even more applicable to Russia that is still searching for its "national self."

---

[20] See, for example, the recent book by Davydov (2002). See also Kulagin 2000; Lebedeva and Mel'vil' 1999.

[21] We specifically refer to Russian debates on modernity and post-modernity (Kapustin 1998, 2001; Neklessa 2000).

[22] The concern from outside the mainstream is, however, that the mainstream theorists, as Ann Tickner (1997) put it, "just don't understand" the significance and the qualitative difference of the post-structuralist agenda.

4. The crisis of self identity: Westernization versus isolationism

Russia's current identity crisis expresses itself through the competition of two often mutually exclusive trends in the country's post-Soviet development, Westernization and isolationism.

Westernization can be defined as active familiarization of Russians with Western theoretical concepts and approaches. It is an important part of the earlier described process of pluralization in the Soviet/Russian IR, and, as such, it contributes greatly to Russian intellectual revival and cultural recovery. For centuries, the West has served as Russia's significant Other, and so long as this will continue to be the case, Russia will be actively borrowing knowledge from this part of the world. As of today, as this volume will illustrate, Russian intellectuals are actively trying out various Western theories. Thus, Shakleyina and Bogaturov describe how Russian IR scholars adopt and modify theories of polarity, and in his earlier work, Bogaturov (1999) makes use of Hedley Bull's theory of International Society. Il'yin writes about Russian responses to Francis Fukuyama's "imperative of modernization" and to Williamson-Kolodko's "Washington consensus." Eduard Solovyev makes clear the influences of traditional European geopolitical theories and Western post-structuralist geography on Russia's emerging geopolitical studies. Stanislav Tkachenko finds it appropriate to apply the American theory of Hegemonic Stability to Russia's post-Soviet conditions. Nayil' Mukharyamov explains the Western origins of Russia's approaches to studying the role of ethnicity in international relations. Finally, Marina Lebedeva demonstrates how Russian negotiation studies developed in close cooperation with those in the West.

Westernization, however, should be distinguished from pluralization. Along with active learning from the Other, Westernization implies Russia's growing dependence on the West's knowledge and—with it—Western cultural values and political ideology. Westernization therefore may come at a cost of delaying or subverting indigineous impulses of epistemological development. Russians are well aware of this cost, as demonstrated by a discussion organized recently by the prominent journal *Pro et Contra*. The discussion's initiator Bogaturov (2000) diagnosed that over the ten post-Soviet years Russian Social Sciences and International Relations progressed within the "paradigm of famil-

iarizing" (*paradigma osvoyeniya*). "Familiarizing" means that after the disintegration of the Soviet Marxist paradigm, many Russian scholars actively
embarked on learning Western theories and methodological apparatuses
partly in order to receive the more readily available and previously inaccessi-
ble Western research grants. But "familiarizing," according to Bogaturov, also
implies a shallow knowledge of Russian realities by the Russians themselves
and a lack of efforts on their part to go beyond fitting these realities into what is
often a straightjacket of alien theoretical concepts. This sounds as a potentially
new version of dogmatism, this time of an anti-Marxist and anti-communist orientation. To respond to the problem, Bogaturov recommends developing a
more indigeneous knowledge:

> Ten years is a considerable time-span. The paradigm of
> familiarizing has served its purpose, but it has also outlived
> itself. Without changing the state of affairs in the Russian
> intellectual community, one cannot avoid undermining the
> authority of knowledge in the eyes of ... younger intellectuals
> ... The time is ripe to study the reality in all of its contradic-
> tions and to build a theory that would cease to view the local
> characteristics as deviations from, and pathologies of, West-
> ern models (Bogaturov 2000).

Western knowledge of course is not homogeneous and may well be open to
cross-cultural engagements if its authors are aware of limitations of their own
cultural contexts and are sensitive to those of others. Some Western theories,
however, allow little room for other cultures. Fukuyama's "end of history" thesis, for instance, implied that the Western values and institutions are the only
ones viable in the world, and that the rest of the human civilization is left to wait
to be absorbed by those values and institutions. Among non-Western audiences, a typical and frequent reaction to this argument is "If history is over,
where are we?" If Western theories (or any other theories for that matter) are
highly ethnocentric, they are likely to meet a resistance or even produce a
nationalistic backlash in alien cultural contexts (Tsygankov 2004).

This takes us to the last and the most unpleasant trend in the Russian IR—
isolation. To a degree, isolation has developed in response to Westernization.
Western knowledge, with its parochial issues and epistemological biases, may

indeed invite rejections and even hostilities. But isolation—a refusal to learn from the Other—also has deep roots in Russia's own superiority/inferiority complex. During the Soviet era, the official Marxism assumed the mantra of speaking on behalf of the "most progressive social class" and therefore, by definition, knowing the "Truth." Post-Soviet IR, alas, is not free from isolationism either. The dangers of isolationism for scholarship are quite obvious. At best, the trend may further delay Russia's answers to its lingering identity questions and slow theory development. At worst, it may resort to the Soviet style propaganda and dogmatism, stiffening any creative indigenous thought.

The works that appear in this issue are illustrative of isolation and its dangers for the new Russian IR. Shakleyina and Bogaturov draw our attention to extreme tendencies in Realist thinking that theorize Russia's rivalry with the West as something "natural" and inevitable. Solovyev describes what may be the strongest candidate to fill the vacancy of the Soviet style isolationism—traditionalist geopolitics. Both extreme Realism and traditionalist geopolitics draw almost exclusively from the 19th-early 20th century geopolitical theories, isolating themselves from contemporary theoretical developments. Russian globalization scholarship, as Il'yin shows, also demonstrates a pattern of isolation when some scholars, for political and ideological reasons, attempt to present the complex phenomenon of globalization as an immoral Western conspiracy against the outside world. Furthermore, Mukharyamov demonstrates how Russian studies of ethnicity are not free of isolationism, with scholars often insisting on ethnically essentialist interpretations of international affairs and attempting no engagement with contemporary Western studies of ethnicity and nationalism. Finally, Lebedeva's study of Russian international negotiations scholarship presents us with yet another version of isolationism in Russian IR. Once a prominent and Westernized area, Russian negotiations studies are increasingly fading away, as scholars are shifting their interests to new issues in the former Soviet region, such as ethnic conflicts.

Overall, isolationism has survived Soviet Marxism because of the persistent legacy of the Russian stigma and identity questions. The old Soviet paradigm has disintegrated, but a new one is only in the process of its emergence. During this process, Russians can use help from the outside world provided that the helpers are free from universalist pretensions of their knowledge. Better solutions would emerge if they are able to guard themselves against the extremes of Westernization and isolationism. Russians should build on their own rich intellectual traditions of both Marxist and non-Marxist varieties. At the same time, they should engage in active dialogue with their IR colleagues in Western and non-Western countries. The resulting knowledge might considerably expand our intellectual horizons.

5. The authors and their contributions

The essays selected for this volume illustrate the above trends and provide the basis for a tentative assessment of the overall growth in Russian IR knowledge.

The three theoretical articles by Alexandr Sergunin, Tatyana Shakleyina and Alexei Bogaturov, and Pavel Tsygankov and Andrei Tsygankov, each describe the progress in Russian theoretical thinking about the world. Sergunin reviews post-Soviet IR discussions and traces how they progressed from one paradigm to another in response to shifts in social issues and political agendas. He concludes that, although realism has emerged as a prominent theoretical paradigm, Russian IR are still in a process of finding their self-definition and remain widely open to various intellectual influences. Shakleyina and Bogaturov study theoretical developments within Russian Realism and evaluate the state of Realist world-order discussions and Russia's strategy after the Cold War. They argue that over the 1990s, Realism has made considerable intellectual progress and has gained the status of a leading intellectual movement in Russia. It assisted the Russian intellectual and political community in defining the country's interests and priorities in the emerging international relations, and it provided a necessary analysis of the world order's structure and polarity.

Finally, Tsygankov and Tsygankov analyze the divisions within Russian Liberalism—another influential IR theory—and the contradictory nature of this intellectual movement. In particular, they draw the attention to the debate between pro-Western and more nationally-oriented liberals, which they propose to understand in terms of the familiar disagreement between supporters of cosmopolitan and communitarian thoughts. Whereas cosmopolitans insist on the emergence of a single humanity and emphasize the factors of unifying and homogenizing nature, communitarians underscore the role of national and cultural foundations in building democratic institutions in the world. The authors trace how various liberal currents understand the nature of the post-Cold War order, Russia's national interests, and its foreign policy orientations.

We have also selected five essays reporting on the progress of specific research programs in Russia. Each of them both confirms and specifies our general assessment of progress in Russian IR development. Studies of globalization and equity have become especially prominent, an encouraging trend in terms of developing original insights and stimulating further research. Building on Stein Rokkan's classification of social cleavages, Mikhayil Il'yin identifies several schools in Russian globalization studies. Namely, he discusses how the distinctions of *authority—people*, *church—state*, *land—industry*, *owners—workers*, *metropolis—colony*, and *network—hierarchy* find their reflection in current Russian research. As Il'yin shows, Russian scholars have recently engaged in a series of discussions of globalization's equity criteria and their application in democratic governance. Inspired by the world system approaches, civilization analysis, and Kondratieff's (1979) cycles, they have articulated series of alternative globalization paths.

Another prominent area of research has been geopolitical studies. Eduard Solovyev of Moscow's Institute of World Economy and International Relations describes the boom that geopolitics has been experiencing after the Soviet breakup. He identifies two main schools of geopolitical analysis, Traditionalism and Revisionism. Traditionalism is inspired by old European and Russian geopolitical theories and views the world through the lense of confrontation over power and resources. Contemporary Russian traditionalists, such the leader of the Communist Party of the Russian Federation Gennadi Zyuganov, also build on dogmatic trends within Soviet Marxism, particularly its extreme determinism. Just as Soviet Marxism sought to justify the "inevitable" victory of the proletariat in the struggle against global capitalism, traditionalist geopolitics confidently predicts the victory of Russian cultural values over those of the West (Zyuganov 1998; Tsygankov 2003b).

The revisionist school, on the other hand, adopts a considerably broader definition of what constitutes geopolitics. Rather than concentrating on power as control of resources, revisionists propose to study various forms of organizing space on a global scale. In contrast to traditionalists, revisionists build on accomplishments of contemporary sociology, critical geography, and political science and make sense of the world in global rather than confrontational terms. In Solovyev's argument, the main problem of contemporary Russian geopolitics is that, while having emerged as a vocation, it is yet to turn into a fully-fledged academic discipline. As of now, geopolitics lacks coherent and scientifically testable theoretical propositions and needs a broad discussion of its issues with the participation of both traditionalists and revisionists. It must also come out of its social science obscurity and enter a dialogue with other disciplines.

Nail' Mukharyamov of Kazan State University focuses on Russian studies of ethnicity, another prominent and distinct area of research. The scholar identifies essentialist and relational approaches that in some ways remind us of the above-made distinction between traditionalist and revisionist geopolitics. Essentialists see the impact of ethnicity as the main organizing force of international politics and posit states as principally ethnocentric units driven by ambitions of large ethnic groups. They see the Russian geographer Lev Gumilev as their intellectual guru, and—because they conceptualize ethnopolitics as the essence of geopolitics—they may be viewed as an extension of geopolitical Traditionalism.

In their turn, relationists question practically all of the essentialist assumptions and seek to depoliticize the notion of ethnicity. Rather than concentrating on states or large ethnic groups in international politics, they take the individual as the main unit of analysis and argue that ethnicity is a choice, not destiny. Their main influence, predictably, comes from Western instrumentalist and constructivist theories of ethnicity and nationalism. Mukharyamov sees both essentialism and relationism as actively developing and associates progress in the field with further development and cross-fertilization of the two ideas. He identifies ethnic conflicts as one the areas in which such cross-fertilization has already emerged and in which scholars have already began to incorporate both structural and relational factors into their analyses.

International Political Economy, however prominent in the West, is not nearly as advanced in Russia. As the St. Petersburg State University scholar

Stanislav Tkachenko argues, Russian IR has not yet established what might be referred to as academic IPE. In the Russian policy community, the main debate is between liberal institutionalists, who advocate the country's integration into the global economy, and the so-called dirigists, who promote relative economic autonomy. These two schools' ideas, however, only begin to find their way into academia. In the authors' view, three main problems impede IPE development in Russian academia — the excessive separation of political science from economics, a deficit of theoretical generalization, and the weakness of the educational curriculum. Tkachenko associates the future of the discipline's development in Russia with solving these three problems. He suggests that as the country continues on the path of economic reform, it is likely to develop the incentive to invest more heavily into IPE as an academic field.

Finally, Marina Lebedeva, currently at the Moscow Institute of International Relations, analyzes progress in yet another field of international relations, international negotiations. Her overall assessment is considerably more pessimistic than those of all other authors writing in this volume. Unlike studies of globalization, geopolitics, or ethnicity, Russian research on negotiations, once a prominent discipline, is currently in decline. Despite the persistent need to study international negotiations, most scholars that had formerly been active in that field have moved to other areas. The rise of new issues demanding urgent attention, the principally changed shape of international negotiations' problematique, as well as serious financial difficulties have all contributed to the discipline's decline. Lebedeva notes that today negotiations remain popular mainly in the field of commercial and business practices. The scholar ends on a positive note and expresses the conviction that international negotiations will be revived as an academic field in Russia. She bases that conviction on the country's practical needs, as well as its growing integration into Western IR studies.

6. Conclusion: toward a better understanding of Russian (and Western) IR

What does the development of Russian IR tell us about the new Russian society? Based on contributions to this issue, one could venture several conclusions. First and foremost, post-communist Russia is a society that is academically open. The meaning of this openness is that all major International Relations traditions—Realism, Liberalism, and Marxism—now exist and develop freely. In this respect, Russia is similar to Western societies; in fact, in some ways, Russia is even more open to broad theoretical discussions because of its incomplete cultural self-definition. Secondly, judging from the same pluralization of international studies, the new Russia is a very diverse society that cannot be restricted to practicing one state-promoted intellectual tradition as it had been under communism. Third, the newly emerged society is more mass-oriented in terms of its social science development. Under communism, International Relations were taught and practiced in one or two elite institutions, such as Moscow Institute of International Relations (MGIMO) and Moscow Diplomatic Academy, and that in no way affected the educational curricula of the rest of the country. Today, international relations, as well as political science, sociology, and other social science disciplines, are in demand throughout the country, and hundreds of specialized departments have opened up and are active in meeting the new demand. Finally, the growth of Russian IR is yet another confirmation that Russians are an outward-looking people. Despite numerous domestic problems, with corruption, street crime, and poverty topping the list, Russians continue to be eager to learn from others, especially from the West. Although the question of how they will apply the learned concepts and theories is still an open one, it is quite clear—thanks in no small measure to IR—that intellectual isolationism is fighting a marginal battle and that mainstream scholars can no longer imagine their development without a dialogue with their foreign colleagues.

Russian IR is not without its problems. One could outline three challenges confronting this new Russian discipline. The first challenge has to do with theory. Many authors of the volume point to the fact that Russian IR remains heavily philosophical, abstract, and detached from empirical scholarship. The second challenge is related to the first, and concerns empirical research. The problem is that genuinely original and indigenous empirical research is still a rare commodity. This, not surprisingly, leads to a lack of middle-level theoretical generalizations, since such generalizations are hard to come by without empirical observations. By building on empirical studies, Russian scholars could generate additional theoretical insights and research programs, thus

contributing to the global field of IR. Last but not least, Russian academia continues to be in a state of financial crisis. To survive, scholars must learn to
swim in waters of both academia and the policy community, and—with salaries
as low as they are—many academics work three to four jobs simultaneously.
How Russian scholars remain engaged in serious research projects under
such conditions remains a mystery to their Western colleagues.

Being mindful of the outlined problems, one can still evaluate the overall
progress of Russian post-Soviet IR as considerable. Despite the limited
resources and time that has passed since the breakup of the hegemonic Marxist paradigm, Russian scholars have managed to develop some original theoretical concepts and research agendas. Although pluralization and
Westernization came at a price, Russians have also made good use of them.
We are therefore cautiously optimistic about the chances of Russian scholarship finding its voice in the global IR community and contributing to stimulating
the discipline's development. The Russian IR community must, of course, continue to fight off the trend of isolationism. The more active Russians are in
communicating across the globe and reflecting back home, the more likely
Russia is to overcome the painful legacy of social stigma and to develop its
own indigenous "Russian school" in global international relations.

The Russian development teaches us another, more general lesson about
the progress of knowledge in Social Science and IR. It suggests that development of global Social Science cannot and should not be a one-sided process,
in which one (the West) teaches and others learn. The world is both global and
culturally pluralist, and that alone assumes the reciprocity of learning. In
George H. Mead's (1967, 271) memorable formulation, "the question whether
we belong to a larger community is answered in terms of whether our own
action calls out a response in this wider community, and whether its response
is reflected back into our own conduct."

Taking this multi-sided and culturally pluralist nature of learning is vital for
our knowledge cumulation and theory building. Without solving this problem,
we make doing research in international studies more difficult because we do
not know if and how far we can extend our knowledge outside its social context. We ought to produce our knowledge with the awareness of the outside
world's possible reactions. Scholarship capable of improving trust and respect

among different cultures and civilizations must be built on the premise that there is both plurality and diversity in the global society. Practically speaking, a good way to overcome the still typical cultural paroichialism in our research is to work together with scholars from different cultures. This would quickly, and positively, affect our disciplinary, methodological, and political biases, and pro- vide a powerful impetus to think differently and think globally. Scholars have never really lived in the "ivory tower," and they can help in building a truly diverse, pluralistic, and multidimensional world. Such is the nature of the world that outside of some commonly agreed-on practices cultural differences will always persist. However, these differences need not be destructive and con- flict-generating; instead, they can and should stimulate dialogue, learning, and creativity.

References

Alker, H. R. and T. J. Biersteker. 1984. The Dialectics of World Order: Notes for a Future Archeologist of International Savior Faire. International Studies Quarterly 28 (2).

Alker, H. R., T. Amin, T. Biersteker, and T. Inoguchi. 1998. How Should We Theorize Contemporary Macro-Encounters: In Terms of Superstates, World Orders, or Civilizations? Paper presented at the Third Pan-European International Relations Conference, SGIR-ISA, Vienna, Austria, September 16-19.

Arbatov, G. A. 1991. Zatyuanuvsheyesya vyzdorovleniye (1955-1985): svidetel'stvo sovremennika. Mezdunarodnyye otnosheniya, Moskva.

Bogaturov, A. 1999. Sindrom poglosheniya v mirovoi politike. Pro et Contra 4 (4).

Bogaturov, A. 2000. Desyat' let paradigmy osvoyeniya. Pro et Contra 5 (4).

Bonker, F., K. Muller, and A. Pickel. 2002. Postcommunist Transformation and the Social Sciences: Cross-Disciplinary Approaches. Rowman & Littlefield, Lanham.

Callahan, W. A. 2003. Nationalizing International Theory: The Emergence of the English School and IR Theory with Chinese Characteristics. Paper presented at the International Studies Association Convention, Portland, Oregon, February.

Crawford, R. M. A. and D. S. L. Jarvis, eds. 2001. International Relations—Still an American Social Science? Toward Diversity in International Thought. State University of New York Press, New York.

Davydov Yu. P. 2002. Norma protiv sily. Problema mirouregulirovaniya. Institut SShA i Kanady, Moskva.

Donaldson, R. H. and J. L. Nogee. 1998. The Foreign Policy of Russia. M. E. Sharpe, Armonk.

English, R. D. 2000. Russia and the Idea of the West. Gorbachev, Intellectuals, and the End of the Cold War. Columbia University Press, New York.

Goffman, E. 1963. Stigma: Notes on the Management of Spoiled Identity. Englewood Cliffs, Prentice-Hall.

Herman, R. G. 1996. Identity, Norms, and National Security: The Soviet Foreign Policy Revolution and the End of Cold War. In The Culture of National Security, edited by P. J. Katzenstein. Columbia University Press, New York.

Hoffmann, S. 1977. An American Social Science: International Relations. Daedalus 106 (3).

Holsti, K.J. 1985. The Dividing Discipline. Hegemony and Diversity in International Theory. Unwin Hyman, Boston.

Hough, J. F. 1986. The Struggle for the Third World: Soviet Debates and American Options. Brookings Institution, Washington, DC.

Inayatullah, N. and D. L. Blaney. 1996. Knowing Encounters: Beyond Parochialism in International Relations Theory. In: The Return of Culture and Identity in IR Theory, edited by Y. Lapid and F. Kratochwil. Lynne Rienner, Boulder.

Kapustin, B. 1998. Sovremennost' kak predmet politicheskoi teorii. ROSSPEN, Moskva.

Kapustin, B. 2001. Postkommunizm kak postsovremennost'. Polis 5.

Klyamkin, I. and L. Shevtsova. 1999. Vnesistemnyi rezhim Borisa II. Carnegie Center, Moscow.

Kolakowski, L. 1978. Main Currents of Marxism. 3 vol. Oxford University Press, Oxford.

Kondratieff, N. D. 1979. The Long Waves of Economic Life. Review II (Spring).

Kubalkova, V. 1992. The Post-Cold War Geopolitics of Knowledge: International Studies in the Former Soviet Bloc. Studies in Comparative Communism 25 (4).

Kubalkova, V. and A. A. Cruickshank. 1985. Marxism and International Relations. Clarendon, Oxford.

Kulagin, V. M. 2000. Mir v XX veke: mnogopolyusnyi balans sil ili global'nyi Pax Democratica. Polis 1.

Lebedeva, M. and A. Mel'vil'. 1999. "Perekhodnyi vozrast" sovremennogo mira. Mezhdunarodnaya zhizn' 10.

Lebedeva, M. 2003. Mirovaya politika. Aspekt-Press, Moskva.

Light, M. 1988. Marxism and Soviet International Relations, Weatsheaf Books, London.

Lynch, A. 1987. The Soviet Study of International Relations. Cambridge University Press, Cambridge.

Marcuse, H. 1958. The Soviet Marxism. New York.

Mead, G. H. 1967. Mind, Self, and Society from the Standpoint of a Social Behaviorist. The University of Chicago Press, Chicago.

Neklessa, A. I. 2000. Ordo Quadro—chetvertyi poryadok: prishestvie postsovremennogo mira. Polis 6.

Neumann, I. B. 1996. Russia and the Idea of Europe. A study in identity and international relations. Routledge, London.

Patomäki, H. and C. Pursiainen. 1999. Western Models and the Russian Idea: Beyond 'Inside/Outside' in Discourses on Civil Society. Millennium 28 (1).

Rajaee, F. 2000. Globalization on Trial. The Human Condition and the Information Civilization. Kumarian Press, Ottawa.

Reddaway, P. and D. Glinski. 2001. The Tragedy of Russia's Reforms: Market Bolshevism against Democracy. The United States Institute of Peace, Washington, DC.

Rupert, M. and H. Smith, ed. 2002. Historical Materialism and Globalization: Essays on Continuity and Change. Routledge, London.

Sakwa, R. 2002. Russian Politics and Society. 3d ed. Routledge, London.

Sergunin, A. A. 2000. Russian post-Communist Foreign Policy Thinking at the Cross-roads. Journal of International Relations and Development 3 (3).

Shakhnazarov, G. 1972. Gryadushchii miroporyadok. Progress, Moskva.

Shakhnazarov, G. 2000. S vozhdyami i bez nikh. Vagrius, Moskva.

Shenfield, S. 1987. The Nuclear Predicament: Explorations in Soviet Ideology. Routledge, London.

Tickner, A. J. 1997. You Just Don't Understand: Troubled Engagements Between Feminists and IR Theorists. International Studies Quarterly 41 (4).

Tolz, V. 2001. Russia: Inventing the Nation. Arnold, London.

Tsygankov, A. P. 2003a. The Irony of Western Ideas in a Multicultural World: Russia's Intellectual Engagements with the "End of History" and "Clash of Civilizations." International Studies Review 8 (1).

Tsygankov, A. P. 2003b. Mastering Space in Eurasia: Russian Geopolitical Thinking after the Soviet Break-Up. Communist and Post-Communist Studies 35 (1).

Tsygankov, A. P. 2004. Whose World Order? Russia's Perception of American Ideas after the Cold War. University Press of Notre Dame, Notre Dame.

Tsygankov, P. A. 2002. Teoriya mezhdunarodnykh otnosheni. Gardarika, Moskva.

Tsygankov, P. A, ed. 1998. Mezhdunarodniye otnosheniya: sotsiologicheskiye podkhody. Gardarika, Moskva.

VTSIOM 2001. Rossiya: zapadniy put' dlia "Yevroaziatskoi" tsivilizatsii..? Vserossiiski tsentr izucheniya obshchestvennogo mneniya (VTSIOM), No. 32 (13 November), http://www.wciom.ru/vciom/new/press/press121115 32.htm, accessed on December 27, 2001.

Waever, O. 1998. The Sociology of a Not So International Discipline: American and European Developments in International Relations. International Organization 52 (4).

Zimmerman, W. 1969. Soviet Perspectives on International Relations, 1956-67. Princeton University Press, Princeton.

Zyuganov, G. 1997. My Russia, edited by V. Meelish, M. E. Sharpe, Armonk.

Zyuganov, G. 1998. Geografiya pobedy. No publisher information, Moskva.

II. Discussions of international relations in post-communist Russia

Alexandr A. Sergunin

1. Introduction

After the demise of the Soviet Union, Russian International Relations (IR) discussions have been highly politicized and centered around political and ideological rather than theoretical issues. There are at least four explanations for why this happened. First, after the collapse of Marxism, the official theoretical basis for the Social Sciences, a sort of theoretical vacuum emerged. For some time, Russian academics simply did not dare to touch on theoretical problems because they were far too sensitive. They were either unable or unwilling to fill the identified vacuum with a new theory or a theory borrowed from abroad. Second, Russian scholars had to respond to the real challenges posed by the post-Cold War international environment and meet the immediate needs that confronted the newly born Russian diplomacy. This environment was more favorable to applied rather than theoretical studies. Third, with the rise of numerous think-tanks and a more or less independent mass media, the demand for foreign policy experts has dramatically increased. Many gifted scholars have moved from academia over to analytical centers, newspapers, and TV programmes or tried to combine these new jobs with their old ones. This has made international studies more popular but their quality and standards of expertise have suffered (Tyulin 1997, 188). Fourth, the chronic economic crisis and changes in public attitudes to science have had a most negative impact on the state of the field in Russia. The state and society as a whole have lost interest in science and higher education and the prestige of these fields have declined accordingly. Salaries have fallen dramatically and social security has been almost destroyed. Scholars have migrated from the academia either abroad or to other sectors (private business, politics, think-tanks, the mass media). According to the Russian Vice-Prime Minister

Vladimir Bulgak, 15,200 Russian scientists have taken up foreign citizenship and another 5,000 are working in foreign countries on a contractual basis (these figures include specialists in natural sciences) (*Rossiyskaya gazeta*, 10 January 1998).

This article distinguishes the main theoretical approaches in the country as they emerged after the 1991. It also outlines the *problematique* of Russian IR discourse.[1] Along with purely Russian schools, almost all of the classic International Relations paradigms—Realism, Idealism/Liberalism and Globalism (or state-centric, multi-centric, and global-centric approaches to international politics) are identified.

2. The Atlanticists ("Westernizers")

The early stage of Russian IR discourse is manifested by the "Atlanticism"-"Eurasianism" dichotomy. Atlanticists were a relatively small but influential group of high-ranking government officials and academics who favoured the pro-Western orientation of Moscow's international strategy. Foreign Minister Andrei Kozyrev became their recognized leader (Arbatov 1993, 9-10; Crow 1993, 22-23), and from August 1991 to the end of 1992, the ideas of this group dominated international discourse in Russia.

The Atlanticists believed that the West (Western Europe and North America) should be the main orientation for Russian diplomacy. They insisted that Russia historically belongs to the Western (Christian) civilization. They saw the main task of Russian international strategy as one of building a partnership with the West and joining Western economic, political, and military institutions—the European Union (EU), North Atlantic Treaty Organization (NATO), International Monetary Fund (IMF), World Bank, Organization for Economic Co-operation and Development (OECD), General Agreement on Tariffs and Trade (GATT), G-7, and so on. Kozyrev stressed that Moscow's main guideline was to join Western democratic states with market economies.

---

[1] The article builds on the author's earlier work on Russian foreign policy and international discussions (Sergunin 2000). For the purpose of concentrating on IR debates, the author omits some other important schools of thinking, such as geopolitics and the imperialist Right, that contributed to the development of Russian foreign policy thinking.

The Atlanticists insisted that Russia should reduce its activities in the former USSR to accommodate its lack of resources, and that radical changes in the country's foreign policy doctrine had to be implemented. They believed that a renunciation of the global imperial policy and the ideological messianism of the former Soviet Union could open up prospects for domestic reforms and facilitate Russia's national revival. At the same time, Moscow could continue to participate in wide-ranging processes of international co-operation (Zagorski et al. 1992, 11).

3. The Eurasianists

"Eurasianism" has emerged as the first serious alternative to the pro-Western theories that were dominant in Russian international thinking during the late 1980s and early 1990s. The "Eurasianist" concept (*yevraziystvo* in Russian) became very popular among Russian intellectuals during the mid-1990s. The concept drew heavily on a philosophical school of 1920s Russian emigres who had tried to find a compromise with the Stalinist version of Socialism. It stresses the uniqueness of Russia. One of its key postulates is that, in civilisational terms, Russia has never been a part of Europe (*Iskhod k Vostoku* 1921; Fedotov 1991; Solonevich 2003). Hence, it should choose a "third way" between the West and the East and attempt to be the bridge between these civilizations.

Contemporary proponents of this theory have been split into two opposing groups. One of them resides in the reformist (so-called "democratic") camp, while the other belongs to the Slavophiles.

The "Democratic" version

The Democrats have tried to adapt Eurasianism to their views for a number of reasons. First, they realized their own weakness stemming from their neglect of Russia's national question and national values. The nationalists and Communists were obviously stronger in this area and were thus in part able to capture the sympathy of ordinary people by appealing to the humiliation of their national dignity. Obviously, the adoption of Eurasianism by the Democrats was part of a strategy aimed at conquering both the public opinion and the political elite. Second, Eurasianism was a reaction among Democrats who were disappointed by both the West's reluctance to admit Russia into its institutions and the small scale of Western assistance to Moscow. They understood that heavy reliance on the West was unwise. By adhering to Eurasianism, they also wanted to send a message that the West could easily lose Russia as a potential ally. Finally, "democratic" Eurasianism reflected the geopolitical position of Russia, or the need to maintain stable relations with both the East and the South. Speaking at a meeting at the Russian Foreign Ministry in February 1992, Sergei Stankevich (1992, 100), the then Advisor to the President, said:

> There is no getting away from certain facts. One of them is that we are now separated from Europe by a whole chain of independent states and find ourselves much further from it. This inevitably involves a definite and, indeed, quite a substantial redistribution of our resources, our potentialities, our links, and our interests in favor of Asia and the Eastern sector.

As apparent from the term "Eurasianism" itself, the geographic frame of reference for the Eurasianist foreign policy concept implied first and foremost the Eurasian continent. Other regions were of peripheral interest for Eurasianism. One observer has put it in pragmatic terms: "the primary object of Russia's mission today is to be fundamental to the stability of the Eurasian continent ... Another aspect of Russia's mission is to guarantee, at least, minimal respect for human rights in the post-Soviet space" (Pleshakov 1993, 22-23). The Eurasianist approach gave priority to the consolidation of economic, political, and security ties between the countries of the FSU, preferably within the context of the Commonwealth of Independent States (CIS) (Travkin 1994, 34-35). The Eurasianists persuaded Yeltsin's government to make the CIS a priority for Moscow's international policy and to initiate the Commonwealth's integration.

The main point in the Eurasianists' dispute with the Atlanticists has been the need to adjust the balance between the Western and Eastern directions of Moscow's international strategy. As one advocate of "democratic" Eurasianism explained, "partnership with the West will undoubtedly strengthen Russia in its relations with the East and South, while partnership with the East and South will give Russia independence in its contacts with the West" (Malcolm 1994, 167).

The Eurasianists recommended co-operation with the Third World rather than with the industrial West (Lukin 1994, 110). While the former perceives Russia as an equal partner, the latter treats Moscow as a "second-echelon" state. In addition, a number of prosperous and rich Asia-Pacific nations such as Japan, South Korea and some of the members of Association of Southeast Asian Nations (ASEAN) are seen as promising trade partners and a source of investment for Russia's troubled economy. Moreover, military co-operation with India and China could serve as important pillars for the new Eurasian security complex (Sergunin and Subbotin 1996a, 3-8; Sergunin and Subbotin 1996b, 24-7).

At the same time, the "democratic" version of Eurasianism has not denied the importance of maintaining good relations with the West. It does not object to Russia entering either economic or "defense structures of the advanced part of the world community" (Bogaturov et al. 1992, 31). In its view, Russia's most important interest consists in improving relations with the European Union and gradual integration into the European economic and political system. At the same time, Russia should oppose the transformation of Europe into a closed economic system and military-political union, just as it should oppose the emergence of a dominant regional power (Germany). For the Eurasianists from the "democratic" camp, it is best to preserve both the multipolar nature of European politics and the role of the United States in the region. Simulta-neously, the school calls for a reconsideration of both the function and the role of NATO (Lukin 1994, 115).

Initially, the "democratic" Eurasianists were much less influential than the Atlanticists within the Yeltsin government and among Russian political elites. However, as the discontent of Russian society with Kozyrev's pro-Western line increased, Eurasianism increased its influence both among the policy-makers and the foreign policy experts. Starting to coalesce in 1992, by 1993 the "Eur-asianist Democrats" were able to influence foreign policy and security debates in Russia.

The Slavophile version

In contrast to the "democratic" version of Eurasianism, the Slavophiles down-played the country's unique geopolitical position and instead stressed Russia's distinctiveness from both the West and the East. El'giz Pozdnyakov (1993a, 6), a Russian authority in International Relations theory, noted:

> The geopolitical location of Russia is not just unique (the same can be said of any state), it is also truly fateful for both herself and the world... An important aspect of this situation [is] that Russia, being situated between two civilizations, [is] a natural holder of both a civilized equilibrium and a world balance of power.

According to the Slavophiles, this geopolitical location predetermined in no small measure the evolution of the Russian state as a great power and the establishment of a strong central authority. Unlike the Democrats, the Slavophiles have not been shy to refer to Russia as an empire and to support the imperial revival (Pozdnyakov 1993b, 30). Contrary to the "Democrats," the Slavophiles did not rule out the use of force to defend Russian minorities in the former Soviet republics. They also opposed Western assistance and proposed to change the current geopolitical priorities by paying more attention to Rus-sia's southern and eastern neighbors.

By the end of 1993, both versions of Eurasianism—"democratic" and Slavophile—found themselves, similar to Atlanticism, in a critical situation because of a number of intellectual and political factors. Other schools of thought, alternatives to both Atlanticism and Eurasianism, became influential at this time.

4. Realism

The rise of realism in Russian IR thinking became possible because of a con-solidation of three major political forces—the industrial lobby, the federal mili-tary and civilian bureaucracies, and the moderate "Democrats." This group was quickly labeled the *derzhavniki* or the *gosudarstvenniki* (proponents of state power). The term *derzhavnik* denotes the advocacy of a strong and powerful state capable of maintaining order and serving as a guarantee against anarchy and instability, a relatively traditional Russian view of the state's role. *Derzhavniki*, with their suspicion towards idealism and romanticism and their advocacy of national interests, paved the way towards the rehabilitation of the Realist school of thought. The balance of power, rather than the balance of interests, was again in fashion. National, not international, security became a matter of primary concern.

Politically, the Realists have belonged to a number of different groups, although the predominant orientation has been towards democratic parties and associations. The Realist concept simply provides them with a common theoretical framework which easily transcends party lines.

According to the Realists, Russia's national security comes first, with the point of departure being the real potential of the state and its ability to take into consideration internal, as well as external, aspects of people's life. In fact, the Realists were one of the first schools in Russia to propose extending the concept of national security to include both "hard" and "soft" security dimensions (Shaposhnikov 1993, 11). In addition, the Realists distinguish between economic, political, social, military, humanitarian, and environmental national interests and sources of threat (National Interests in Russian Foreign Policy 1996, 8). They stress that, in an interrelated and interdependent world, national interests of different countries may overlap, cross, or even clash in various forms, ranging from "soft" or diplomatic clashes to "hard" or military ones.

The Realists also distinguish two kinds of threats to Russia's security: external and internal. External political threats include attempts to challenge the territorial integrity of the Russian Federation, blocking of integration processes in the CIS, political instability in neighboring countries, and efforts to weaken Russia's role and position in international organizations. Economic threats include Russia's diminished economic independence and scientific potential, as well as its diminished presence in some of the world's markets. Among external military threats, the Realists list armed conflicts in the proximity of Russia, nuclear proliferation, and lack of proper borders, especially in the south and west of Russia. In addition, the Realists identify threats of environmental (ecological disasters in neighboring countries and long-term negative effects resulting from global environmental shifts) and social (internationalization of organized crime, drug trafficking, international terrorism, mass epidemics, and so on) nature (Shaposhnikov 1993, 14-18; Kokoshin 2002).

However, the Realists were also keen to emphasize that the present main sources of threat to Russia's security come from the country's deep internal crisis. Some realists described the internal threats as follows (Shaposhnikov 1993, 14-18; Lukov 1995, 5-7):

(a)   a potential disintegration of the Russian Federation as a result of inter-ethnic and centre/regions conflicts;

(b)   socio-economic tensions stemming from economic decline, the rupture of economic ties, inflation, rising unemployment, deep social differentiation, the degradation of science, the education system, medical services, and so on;

(c)   organized crime and corruption;

(d)   cultural and spiritual degradation;

(e)   degradation of the environment; and

(f)   lack of information security.

To cope with these threats, the Realist recommend that Russia first completes its domestic reforms. Only then will the country have the necessary resources to restore its internal and some of its external stability. Among other tools, the Realists prefer political, diplomatic, economic, and other peaceful methods to meet security challenges. However, they do not rule out the use of military force if differences between states' vital interests cannot be reconciled (National Interests in Russian Foreign Policy 1996, 9-10).

The regional priorities of the Realists are similar to those of the Eurasianists. Rogov (1993, 76) suggests that there are three main circles of Russian interests—(1) "near abroad," (2) East Europe, the Middle East and Far East, and (3) the West (the United States and Western Europe). The rest of the world is viewed as of peripheral importance.

Similarly to the Eurasianists, the Realists have stressed the Eurasian geopolitical location of Russia (Rogov 2000b). However, they argue that Russian foreign policy on the continent should be defined by real interests rather than messianic ideas. For example, according to Lukin, in the years ahead Russia will have to vigorously resist Islamic fundamentalism, the spread of which would threaten to destabilize the situation both near and inside the CIS. Still, it is essential not to be drawn into a confrontation with the biggest Islamic countries (including Iran), but instead to seek various avenues of agreement and to develop mutually beneficial interstate relations. In addition, Russia must rebuff all attempts by Turkey, Pakistan and Afghanistan to encroach on Russian economic, political, and military interests.

In Europe, the Realists opposed the expansion of NATO, which they view as detrimental to the regional security system and Russia's security. While acknowledging the Alliance's positive role in European security (Arbatov 1999), the Realists argue in favor of the OSCE as the main collective security organization on the continent (Arbatov 1995). They have pointed to the Kosovo crisis as evidence of the threat emanating from the NATO-centric European security model (Arbatov 1999, 8; Pyadyshev 1999, 2).

Believers in the balance of power system, the Realists are especially wary of China. They warn of the possibility of Russia's one-sided dependence on China in case of Moscow's rapprochement with Beijing (Trush 1996, 4) and argue that the country's interests may best be served by the maintenance of America's political role and limited military presence in the region. In addition to maintaining a US military presence, Russia's national interests would best be served by developing a new multilateral security system in the region. Russia and the West have common interests in reforming Russian economic and political system, maintaining an arms control regime, preventing the rise of revisionist regional powers, and peace-keeping (Rogov 1995, 2000a). At the same time, Russia should be firm as regards to its most vital interests: preservation of a common European security system, maintaining a dominant position in the post-Soviet area, or arms sales to the Third World (Rogov 2000a).

September 11 was seen by Russian Realists as the return of the 19th century-like world, in which selfish national interests prevail and international organizations are unable to prevent the spread of violence, which confirmed the Realists' view that Russia should be prepared to build and shift coalitions according to its national interests (Andrusenko and Tropkina 2002; Satanovsky 2003). The Realists approvingly point to Russia's cooperation with the United States in Afghanistan and Russia's alliance with France and Germany over Iraq as examples of such *ad hoc* coalitions and believe that Russia should also work on strengthening international collective decision-making bodies, such as the G-8 and the UN Security Council (Dmitriyeva 2003b; Lukin 2003). Some of them continue to believe in a multipolar world order and in counterbalancing American superpower (Lukin 2003; Suslov 2003), while others see no alternative to US unipolarity and recommend that Russia sides with the United States as a junior partner (Dmitrieva 2003a).

The Realist legacy has had a fairly mixed record. On the one hand, Realism has contributed positively to Russian international debate. The Realists have helped to overcome the crisis in Russian foreign policy thinking which had been generated by the struggle between two powerful extremes represented by Atlanticism and Eurasianism. The Realists succeeded in articulating Russia's real security interests and priorities to both domestic and foreign audiences. Moreover, the spread of their ideas made Russian security thinking more predictable and understandable for the West. The new Russian national security concept, approved by the President in December 1997 (and revised in January 2000), drew heavily upon realist ideas (*Kontseptsiya natsionalnoi bezopasnosti Rossiyskoi Federatsiyi* 1997, 4-5). On the other hand, the Realist emphasis on national interests, national security, and national sovereignty implied an obvious return to the old paradigm of classical modernity. Realism failed to develop any concepts for addressing the challenges of the post-modern world.

5. The Liberal paradigm

Despite the dominance of the Realist/geopolitical paradigm, the Idealist/Liberal perspective on international relations is also represented in Russia. In fact, the Atlanticists drew upon some Idealist principles. Idealism emphasizes globalization trends in the world economy which strengthen the trend toward global management of economic and political developments and generally increases the relevance of international legal frameworks, thus reducing global anarchy. Idealists believe that the development of multilateral institutions and regimes could guarantee stability of the international system. Although the trend toward a multipolar world is not neglected within the Idealist/Liberal perspective, it argues that the future development of the international system is no longer predominantly determined by the shape and outcome of rivalries among the major centers of economic and military power but rather by the dynamics of their common development and interdependence (Khrustalev 1992; Zagorski et al. 1992, 5-13). The Idealists/Liberals argue that the geopolitical drive for control over territories no longer matters and suggest that it should be replaced by geoeconomic thinking (Zagorski 1995a, 5-8; Neklessa 2000).

The debate between the Realists and Idealists on more practical aspects of diplomacy was especially visible on two issues: CIS integration and European security. The Liberals (Zagorski 1995b, 263-70; Lebedeva and Mel'vil' 1999) argue that Russia's real dilemma in the CIS is not disintegration versus integration but rather the challenge of successfully completing democratic and market reforms in the region. As for European security, the Liberal basic argument has been that Russia's predominant interest in Europe should be the strengthening of multilateral institutions which would then serve as a guarantee against the return to balance of power politics (Tyulin 1997, 187). The group saw no serious threat stemming from NATO enlargement and views it as a natural reaction Russia's unpredictable behavior. The Liberals criticized Yeltsin for his inability to fully use the opportunities presented by non-NATO security arrangements that ranged from PfP (Partnership for Peace) to OSCE program (Kortunov 1996, 74-75). Moreover, many liberals consider NATO as the main guarantor of stability in Europe and as an alliance of democracies that has defensive rather than offensive intentions (Kortunov 1996). Russia's threats are seen as mainly internal, having to do with economic decline, organized crime, environmental decay, and domestic separatism. Liberals view NATO's military intervention in Yugoslavia as an overreaction to Milosevic's policies, but insist that Russia should nonetheless view NATO as the key partner in ensuring European security (Orlov 1999, 15; Trenin 1999).

The Realists and Idealists, therefore, disagree on the nature of the post-Cold War order. Realists believe that in an age of multipolarity, only a flexible pan-European security system, such as OSCE, can guarantee a balance of power on the continent and protect the national sovereignty of Russia and other countries. The Liberals, on the other hand, were quite pessimistic of effectiveness pan-Europeanism and saw a "Big Europe" emerging as a result of the expansion of the West European and trans-Atlantic institutions (Zagorski 1996, 67; Trenin 1999). Russia's main policy objective should be integration into the world economy and the community of democratic states (Kulagin 2000), which can only be attained through cooperation with NATO and other European organizations. Russian Liberals have also expressed their concerns about the rise of unilateral politics and the decreasing role of international organizations in the aftermath of 9-11 (Volkov 2003).

Although the Liberals have been unable to dominate or seriously influence Russia's international discourse, they perform a useful role by challenging Realism/Eurasianism and serving as an intellectual alternative to power thinking.

6. The Neo-Marxists

There are two main versions of Marxist-inspired political thought in Russia. The first is more traditional and is exemplified by the Communist Party of the Russian Federation (CPRF), led by Gennadi Zyuganov. The second one lies closer to social democracy and has been developed by some non-governmental organizations, such as the Gorbachev Foundation.

Traditionalists

The Communists have been unable to reconcile themselves to the demise of the Soviet Union and to the country's loss of great power status. They believe that Gorbachev and Yeltsin led USSR to its defeat in the Cold War and to its subsequent collapse. The Communists commonly view these leaders as national traitors (Elections 1995, 7).

As some pro-Communist experts have suggested, Russia has two alternatives for a national security doctrine—(a) the domination of national-state interests over cosmopolitan ones, and Russia's independent position in the international relations system; or (b) the orientation towards Western values and the joining of a "community of civilized countries" (Podberezkin 1996, 86). The CPRF opted for the first alternative. The Communists emphasized the invariable nature of the country's national interests which they regard as independent of a political regime or a dominant ideology. They believed that Russia's main historical national interest lied in preserving its territorial and spiritual integrity. The idea of a powerful state based on multi-ethnicity was equivalent to the Russian national idea. Thus, the breakdown of the Soviet Union and weakening of the Russian state have undermined Russian security and worsened its geostrategic position. The Communists also acknowledged the need for a national idea or doctrine that could help consolidate Russian society (Podberezkin 1995, 89; Zyuganov 1998, 42-49).

As for threat perceptions, the Communists believe that the breakdown of the Warsaw Pact, the withdrawal of Russian troops from Eastern Europe, and the loss of Moscow's control over this region have generated new threats to Russia's security (Zyuganov 1998, 72-77). NATO's eastward expansion further violated the strategic balance in Europe. The Kosovo intervention was a "natural" result of NATO's enlargement, and Kosovo-like operations could be repeated on the territory of the CIS space and even Russia (Guseinov 1999, 4). Pro-Communist analysts have also singled out global developments that could challenge Russian national security. These include:

(1) resurgent powers that aim to change their regional and global status, thus shifting the global power balance (Germany, Japan, China, India, Brazil, South Africa, and others);

(2) the rise of regionalism in the world (EU, NAFTA, ASEAN, etc.), which could potentially increase Russia's isolation;

(3) the aggravation of global social, economic and environmental problems; and

(4) a decrease in the significance of nuclear deterrent force and the rise of unstable regional alliances with high conflict potential (Podberezkin 1996, 88).

In terms of regional priorities, the Communists, similarly to the Eurasianists, regard the CIS and "near abroad" as the first priority for Moscow. They believe that the Soviet Union has been dissolved illegally and have tried to foster the reunification of the former Soviet republics. Even so, they have ruled out the use of force to restore the USSR. According to Zyuganov, the Soviet restoration should be conducted on a "voluntary basis" (Zyuganov 1995, 86). Along with some liberals and nationalists, the Communists have put pressure on the Yeltsin government to protect Russian minorities abroad.

The Realists in principle agree with the Communists on their assessment of the implications of NATO's enlargement and the Kosovo war. However, they do not view NATO member-states as completely united with regard to enlargement and the necessity of humanitarian interventions in the world. They believe in the possibility of a compromise between the Alliance and Russia that would guarantee Moscow's security and minimize the enlargement's negative effects (Rogov 1997, 9; Arbatov 1999).

The Communists have also proposed that Russia restore its ties with its "traditional friends and allies," such as Iraq, Libya, North Korea, and Cuba, in order to prevent America's unchallenged world-wide leadership and to provide Russia with additional markets for its troubled arms industry. It should be noted, however, that despite its immense domestic influence, the CPRF has been unable to seriously influence Russian IR discussions.

The Social Democrats

After his resignation in December 1991, Mikhail Gorbachev and a number of his close friends—Alexandr Yakovlev and Georgi Shakhnazarov being the most prominent among them—committed themselves to the creation of a social-democratic movement in Russia in opposition to both the communist-nationalist coalition and the monetarists. The Gorbachev Foundation and the journal *Svobodnaya mysl'* (Free Thought) became the most important platforms for the rise of social democracy in Russia.

Similar to the Eurasianists, the social democratic security thinking has focused on the concept of stability. Internal stability has been defined as cohesion within the political system, adherence to normal democratic procedures in the rotation of ruling elites, the absence of pressing ethnic and social conflicts, and a healthy, functioning economy (Bogomolov 1994, 142). International stability has been seen as the balance of interests among major international players (contrary to the balance of power idea popular in the past) (Kolikov 1994, 12).

Along with other schools of thought, the Social Democrats have contributed to the Russian discussion on national interests. Contrary to the Gorbachev doctrine, which stressed the unconditional priority of "all-human" interests over national interests, the Social Democrats have acknowledged that national interests are the subject of primary concern for any country. They defined national interests as a manifestation of the nation's basic needs (survival, security, progressive development) (Krasin 1996, 5).

The Social Democrats, however, do not limit themselves to the acknowledgement of national interests' significance. They also believe that in an interdependent world, international actors cannot afford to solely pursue their own interests. Since the international environment has become multi-dimensional, the actors should take into account both the national interests of other players and the universal (all-human) interests (Kuvaldin 2000). According to the Social Democrats, narrow-minded nationalism is absolutely outdated and detrimental not only to the world community but also to the nation conducting a policy in the interests of the nation (Utkin 1995). They realize that democracy in the international system is still in its infancy, and that few "all-human" values have taken root in humankind's mentality. The Social Democrats regarded the creation of a global civil society as the only way to replace national interests with "all-human" values. In their view, a world civil society could be based on a system of horizontal links between inter-government and non-government organizations dealing with economic, political, environmental, and cultural issues (Krasin 1996, 12). Some experts have proposed the creation of a world government to resolve global problems and to save humankind from imminent catastrophe (Shakhnazarov 1996, 79; Kuvaldin 2000). Thus, the Kantian (1957) project of "eternal peace"—the methodological basis of the New Political Thinking and its current proponents—could be put into practice.

The Social Democrats perceive the world as moving from a unipolar, with the United States as the only superpower, towards a multipolar structure. None of the countries or ideologies will be able to impose its model on others. The Social Democrats disagrees with Fukuyama's (1992) thesis on the world-wide domination of the liberal-democratic model. Various civilizational models will compete in the foreseeable future. A future world will be born in the process of interaction between two contradictory processes—integration and regionalization. The future power poles will emerge on the basis of economic, religious, and cultural differentiation. Some analysts distinguish Arab-Muslim, Europe-centric (including the United States), Eurasian (including Eastern Europe), South Atlantic, Indian, and Asia-Pacific centers (Dakhin 1995, 85).

Which identity should Russia choose? The Social Democrats usually pay tribute to the Eurasian geographical position of the country, but they empha-size that, from a cultural and civilizational point of view, Russia is a part of Europe (Gorbachev 1992; Kolikov 1994, 5; Maksimychev 1997). For that rea-son, Russia should aim at entering pan-European economic, political, and security structures. "Europe" is also defined in a civilizational rather than geo-graphical sense: the Gorbachevian project of a Common European House or "Europe from Vancouver to Vladivostok" is still popular among the Russian Social Democrats.

7. Postmodernism in Russia

Up until now, Russian scholarship has been quite indifferent to postmodernism as a school of Western political thought. The Russian academic community has mainly ignored both the postmodern *problematique* and the discussions around it. Indeed, many Russian theorists are not even aware of this particular school (Sergunin and Makarychev 1999). Some, however, have suggested that certain postmodern insight could be well received in Russia because of its national characteristics. For example, Russians have never been fully satisfied with the project of modernity grounded in rationalism, a belief in linear progress and the decisive role of scientific knowledge. They have also been open to dialogue with other civilizations and cultures.

There is growing feeling among some Russian scholars that the country has already entered the postmodern epoch (Kapustin 2001). There are com-pletely new temporal and spatial dimensions in which individuals and society live in the period of transition. Moral values and individual perceptions of the surrounding world have changed significantly as well. At the same time, Rus-sia's economic and technological potential, social structure, and political sys-tem still have their roots in modernity. This typically postmodern discrepancy between an individual's material conditions and the psychological and spiritual orientations is emerging as a fashionable theme in Russian social science literature (Busygina 1995, 5-9; Kachanov 1995, 38; Panarin 2000). Postmodernist thought has had some influence on Russian IR discourse—at least in the studies of world order and foreign policy. For example, Il'yin (1995, 48-9), while rejecting the idea of postmodernity, offers a relatively postmodern worldview by describing the present system of international relations as a combination of nation-states with "post-urbanist mutations of civilizations" and "global villages"/"choritikas" (from Greek "choritika"—rural, country, territorial). The latter he interprets as transterritorial, transnational, and global political systems based on telecommunications and political rhetoric.

Some Russian scholars borrow the grammatological civilizational model from Western poststructuralists to explain the causes of conflict between different nations and civilizations. According to this model (Kuznetsov, 1995:98-9), a system of writing is a more important civilizational link between members of a nation than religion or culture. Present-day Russia, for instance, is a rather loose formation from a religious point of view, but, in terms of writing (Cyrillic alphabet), it is relatively homogeneous. In contrast to Hungtington's "clash of civilizations" theory, these scholars analyze ethnic conflicts as grounded in a "war of alphabets": Serbs vs. Croats (Cyrillic vs. Latin alphabet); Armenians vs. Azeri in Nagorny Karabakh (Armenian vs. switching to the Latin alphabet); Greek vs. Turks in Cyprus (Greek vs. Latin alphabet); Russians vs. Chechens (Cyrillic vs. switching to the Latin alphabet).

As to security issues, Russian postmodernists argue against the concept of national interests, which they view as a "conservative utopia" and a mere camouflage for parochial interests. In reality, the so-called national interests reflect neither a state's nor a nation's interests, but instead are interests of the ruling elite. By imposing its perception of national interests on society, the ruling elite tries to legitimize its dominance and control over both state and society. Each stratum or group has its own vision of "national interests," but only the one followed by the most powerful group becomes officially recognized. Therefore, foreign policy based on quasi-national interests can be detrimental to a significant part of society (Kapustin 1996, 16-19).

Postmodernist scholars view the revival of Realism in Russia and other countries as a "primitive communitarian response" to the dominance of universalism in the age of modernity, brought to humankind by the Enlightenment. An insistence on the exclusiveness of national interests could result in endless confrontation with other international actors and divert the country away from its democratic path (Kapustin 1996, 28). In the age of the transnational economy, information, and communications, Russian postmodernists recommend strengthening new universal norms of multi-culturalism, tolerance, self-criticism, and dialogue (Kapustin 1996, 28).

It is hard to see postmodernists becoming influential in Russian IR in the foreseeable future. There are at least three main obstacles to the growth of their influence. First, Russia is still at the stage of trying to define its own national identity and, therefore, Realist concepts of national interests, national security, power balance and so forth will remain attractive for both academics and policy planners for many years to come. Second, in restricting themselves to "deconstruction," postmodernists are unable to produce any new theory and in fact oppose the very idea of theorizing. Finally, Western postmodernism had already passed its peak in the late 1980s-early 1990s and therefore might have missed its best opportunity to gain a following in Russia.

Nonetheless, as Russia continues to progress with its reforms and opens up to greater international co-operation, it will have to address the postmodern *problematique*. Adequate responses to postmodern challenges will not necessarily be found within the Western-like postmodernist tradition; they might be developed by representatives of other theoretical schools. One way or another, these challenges must be met; otherwise Russia may never be revived as competitive and prosperous nation.

8. Conclusions

Six conclusions could be drawn from the above analysis. First, Russian international studies have experienced a very quick and dramatic transformation from a discipline dominated by Marxist ideology to a multiparadigmatic discourse. Second, despite the early polarization of Russian IR debates, many schools have now agreed on some common principles, a development partially stemming from Western interventionist practices in the Balkans and elsewhere. These principles include the priority of national interests, an active foreign policy, domestic reform, and security protection. Realism has played a prominent role in outlining these principles as Russia's *modus operandi*. Third, although the Realist school currently dominates the discipline, other perspectives (such as Idealism/Liberalism, globalism and post-positivism) do exist and do present alternatives to the dominant paradigm. It appears that, in the foreseeable future, Russian foreign policy discourse will resemble polyphony rather than monophony or cacophony. Fourth, two main topics — diplomatic history and contemporary Russian foreign policy — are the most popular themes among Russian scholars and analysts. Russian authors have taken great strides in exploring these problems. However, the country's scholarship continues to lack profound theoretical works in this field. Fifth, international studies has ceased to be an elitarian discipline and has become a more "normal" one. Finally, the "democratization," "demonopolization" and "normalization" of international relations has had many implications at the institutional level: the number of research centers dealing with international studies has dramatically increased, and new regional centers have emerged. This has made Russian scholarship even more diverse and interesting.

References

Andrusenko, L. and O. Tropkina. 2002. Mezalyans s Amerikoi. Nezavisimaya gazeta, 11 September.

Arbatov, A. 1993. Russia's Foreign Policy Alternatives. International Security 18 (2).

Arbatov, A. 1995. Rossiya i NATO. Nezavisimaya gazeta, 9 June.

Arbatov, A. 1999. NATO kak glavnaya problema yevropeiskoi bezopasnosti. Nezavisimaya gazeta, 16 April.

Bogaturov, A., M. Kozhokin, K.Pleshakov. 1992. Vneshnyaya politika Rossiyi. SShA: economika, politica, ideologiya 25 (10).

Bogomolov, O. T. 1994. Russia and Eastern Europe. In: Damage Limitation or Crisis? edited by Robert D. Blackwill and Sergei A. Karaganov. Brassey's, Washington, DC and London.

Busygina, I. M. 1995. Postmodernizm v Moskve. Polis 6.

Crow, S. 1993. The Making of Foreign Policy in Russia under Yeltsin. Radio Free Europe/Radio Liberty Research Institute. Munich and Washington, DC.

Dakhin, V. 1995. Kontury novogo mira. Svobodnaya mysl' 4.

Dmitriyeva, O. 2003a. Plyusy odnogo polyusa. Rossiyskaya gazeta, 20 May.

Dmitriyeva, O. 2003b. "Vosmyerka" budet pravit' mirom? Rossiyskaya gazeta, 31 May.

Elections. 1995. Parties' Foreign Policy Views. International Affairs (Moscow) 41 (11-2).

Fedotov, G. P. 1911. Sud'ba i grekhi Rossiyi. Vol. 1-2. St. Paleya, Petersburg.

Fukuyama, F. 1992. The End of History and the Last Man. Penguin Books, Harmondsworth.

Gorbachev, M. 1992. Epilogue. In: Europe by Nature, edited by Bento Bremer. Van Gorcum, Assen.

Guseinov, V. 1999. Obnovleniye NATO i bezopasnost' Rossii. Nezavisimoye voennoe obozorenie, 16-22 April.

Il'yin, M. V. 1995. Ocherki khronopoliticheskoi tipologii. MGIMO, Moskva.

Iskhod k Vostoku. 1921. Rossiisko-Bolgarskoe knigoizdatelstvo, Sofia.

Kachanov, Y. 1995. Politicheskaya topologiya: strukturirovaniye politicheskoi realnosti. Nauka, Moskva.

Kant, I. 1957. Perpetual Peace. Bobbs-Merill Company, Indianapolis and New York.

Kapustin, B. 1996. "Natsionalnyi interes" kak konservativnaya utopiya. Svobodnaya mysl' 3.

Kapustin, B. 2001. Postkommunizm kak postsovremennost'. Polis 5.

Khrustalev, M. A. 1992. After the Disintegration of the Soviet Union: Russia in a New World. MGIMO, Moskva.

Kokoshin, A. A. 2002. Fenomen globalizatsii i interesy natsional'noi bezopasnosti. In: Vneshnyaya politika i bezopasnost' sovremennoi Rossii. 1991-2002, Vol. 1, edited by Tatyana Shakleyina, ROSSPEN, Moskva.

Kolikov, N. 1994. Rossiya v kontekste globalnykh peremen. Svobodnaya mysl' 2-3.

Kontseptsiya natsionalnoy bezopasnosti Rossiyskoy Federatsii. 1997. Rossiyskaya gazeta, 26 December.

Kontseptsiya natsionalnoy bezopasnosti Rossiyskoi federatsiyi. 2000. Nezavisimoye voennoye obozreniye, 14-20 January.

Kortunov, A. 1996. NATO Enlargement and Russia. In: Will NATO Go East? edited by David G. Haglund. Queen's University, Kingstone.

Krasin, Yu. 1996. Natsionalnye interesy: mif ili realnost'? Svobodnaya mysl' 3.

Kulagin, V. M. 2000. Mir v XX veke: mnogopolyusnyi balans sil ili global'nyi Pax Democratica. Polis 1.

Kuvaldin, V. B. 2000. Globalizatsiya—svetloye buduscheye chelovechestva? NG-stsenarii 9, 11 October.

Kuznetsov, A. 1995. A New Model for Traditional Civilizations. International Affairs (Moscow) 41 (4-5).

Lebedeva, M. and A. Mel'vil'. 1999. "Perekhodnyi vozrast" sovremennogo mira. Mezhdunarodnaya zhizn' 10.

Lukin, V. 1994. Russia and its Interests. In: Rethinking Russia's National Interests, edited by Stephen Sestanovich. Center for Strategic and International Studies, Washington, DC.

Lukin, V. 2003. Prishla pora igrat' v komandnuyu igru. Nezavisimaya gazeta, 24 March.

Lukov, V. 1995. Russia's Security: The Foreign Policy Dimension. International Affairs (Moscow) 41 (5).

Makarychev, A. S. and A. A. Sergunin. 1996. Postmodernizm i zapadnaya politicheskaya nauka. Sotsialno-politicheskiyi zhurnal 15 (3).

Maskimychev, I. F. 1997. Rossiya kak sostavnaya chast' obscheyevropeiskogo tsivilizatsionnogo protranstva. Obschestvennyye nauki i sovremennost' 6.

Malcolm, N. 1994. New Thinking and After. In: Russia and Europe: An End to Confrontation? edited by Neil Malcolm. Pinter, London and New York.

National Interests in Russian Foreign Policy. 1996. International Affairs (Moscow) 42 (2).

Neklessa, A. I. 2000. Ordo Quadro—chetvertyi poryadok: prishestivye postsovremennogo mira. Polis 6.

Orlov, B. 1999. Pochemu Nezavisimaya gazeta protiv NATO? Nezavisimaya gazeta, 23 April.

Panarin, A. S. 2000. Global'noye politicheskoye prognozirovaniye. Algoritm, Moskva.

Pleshakov, K. 1993. Russia's Mission: the Third Epoch. International Affairs (Moscow) 39 (12).

Podberezkin, A. 1995. Cherez dukhovnost—k vozrozhdeniyu otechestva. Svobodnaya mysl' 5.

Podberezkin, A. 1996. Geostrategicheskoe polozhenie i bezopasnost' Rossii. Svobodnaya mysl' 7.

Pozdnyakov, E. 1993a. Russia is a Great Power. International Affairs (Moscow) 39 (1).

Pozdnyakov, E. 1993b. Russia Today and Tomorrow. International Affairs (Moscow) 39 (2).

Pyadyshev, B. 1999. Novy tsentr mirovoi vlasti. Nezavisimaya gazeta, 5 November.

Rogov, S. 1995. Russia and the United States: A Partnership or Another Disengagement. International Affairs (Moscow) 41 (7).

Rogov, S. 1997. Dogovor podpisan, problemy ostayutsya. Literaturnaya gazeta, 28 May.

Rogov, S. 2000a. Rossiya i SShA na poroge XXI veka. Dipkur'yer NG, 6 April.

Rogov, S. 2000b. Izolyatsiya ot integratsii. Dipkur'yer NG, 7 December.

Satanovsky, Ye. 2003. Nastupaet ocherednoi peredel mira. Nezavisimaya gazeta, 24 March.

Sergounin, A. and S. Subbotin. 1996a. Indo-Russian Military Co-operation: Russian Perspective. Asian Profile, February.

Sergunin, A. and S. Subbotin. 1996b. Sino-Russian Military Co-operation and Evolving Security System in East Asia. University of Nizhny Novgorod, Nizhniy Novgorod.

Sergunin, A. and A. Makarychev. 1999. Sovremennaya zapadnaya politicheskaya mysl': postpozitivistskaya revolyutsiya. Nizhniy Novgorod Linguistic University Press, Nizhniy Novgorod.

Shakhnazarov, G. 1996. Vostok i Zapad: samoidentifikatsiya na perelome vekov. Svobodnaya mysl' 8.

Shaposhnikov, Ye. 1993. A Security Concept for Russia. International Affairs 39 (10).

Solonevich, I. 2003. Narodnaya monarchiya. Paleya, Moskva.

Stankevich, S. 1992. A Transformed Russia in a New World. International Affairs 38 (4-5).

Suslov, D. 2003. Voina v Irake ne povliyala na polozheniye Rossii v mire. Nezavisimaya gazeta, 21 April.

Travkin, N. 1994. Russia, Ukraine, and Eastern Europe. In: Rethinking Russia's National Interests, edited by Stephen Sestanovich. Center for Strategic and International Studies, Washington, DC.

Trenin, D. 1999. Realpolitik i realnyaya politika. Nezavisimoye voennoye obozrenyie, 1-7 October.

Trush, S. 1996. Prodazha rossiyiskogo oruzhiya Pekinu: rezony i opaseniya. Nezavisimaya gazeta, 25 April.

Tyulin, I. G. 1997. Between the Past and the Future: International Studies in Russia. Zeitschrift für Internationale Beziehungen 4 (1).

Volkov, A. 2003. Bez suda i sledstviya. Rossiyskaya gazeta, 18 March.

Utkin, A. 1995. Natsionalizm i buduschee mirovogo soobshchestva. Svobodnaya mysl' 3.

Zagorski, A. 1995a. Was für eine GUS erfüllt ihren Zweck? Aussenpolitik 46 (3).

Zagorski, A. 1995b. Geopolitik versus Geowirtschaft. Wostok 5(6).

Zagorski, A. 1996. Russia and Europe. Romanian Journal of International Affairs 2 (1-2).

Zagorski, A, A. Zlobin, S. Solodovnik, and M. Khrustalev. 1992. Russia in a New World. International Affairs (Moscow) 38 (7).

Zyuganov, G. 1995. Za gorizontom. Veshniye vody, Orel.

Zyuganov, G. 1998. Geografiya pobedy. No publisher, Moskva.

III. The Russian Realist school of international relations

Tatyana A. Shakleyina and Alexei D. Bogaturov

1. Introduction

This article analyzes the Realist school in the Russian international relations scholarship and discusses the debates among Russian Realists. Although Russian Realists are not a homogeneous group, they are united by the questions they discuss. Their main issues of focus are the characteristics of the newly-emerging world order and the development of an adequate strategy for Russia to pursue in its international behavior. Many Realists, as well as Liberals, are convinced of the current world's unipolar nature. However, while Russian Liberals view democratic institutions and norms as the pillar of the world order[1], realists put emphasis on power centers (poles), using this perspective to describe the emerging international system[2].

In the first half of the 1990s, Russia's foreign policy was not directed toward support of the balance of power in international relations, and Realism was not dominant in Russian discussions of the world's future and the country's strategy. However, in the second half of the 1990s and especially in early XXI century, the idea of balance of power reemerged in official rhetoric and foreign policy discussions. Russia's role and strategy began to be defined in terms of supporting a multipolar balance of power in the world. Unlike many American Realists, the majority of Russian Realists view unipolarity of the international

---

[1] One of the leading representatives of Russian Liberal IR is Yuri P. Davydov. In his book *Norms against Power* (2002), he outlines three types of world order—unipolar, bipolar, and functional, the latter being the objective of Western democracies after the Cold War. In his view, the key characteristics of the functional world order are the strengthening of interdependence and globalization processes, the rising role of non-governmental organizations in foreign policies, and the decline of the role of state in international policy making (Davydov 2002, 41-42).

[2] By "pole" (*polyus*), Russian scholars often mean a power center with considerable potential (military, economic, political, etc.) and desire or will to regulate world processes.

system as problematic and harmful, although many of them acknowledge the necessity to accept it. Today, most Russian scholars and politicians insist that the new Russia must become a part of the emerging world order on most favorable terms possible. This shift in discourse should be viewed as a victory of Realism in Russian debates on international relations.

2. Russian Realism: approaches and issues

Realism in international relations means the analysis of world politics from the point of view of existing conflicts and contradictions. Unlike Liberals, who point to possibilities for achieving international agreements and cooperation, Realists emphasize principal differences of interests among major actors of world politics. The Soviet-era roots of Russian Realism are described in more detail below.

2.1. Theoretical approaches

Realism in Russia does not represent a single direction or unified methodological approach. Disagreements inside realism relate to various spheres and are often rather deep. However, it is possible to identify six methodological traditions which have emerged in post-Soviet Russia.

Historical systemic approaches

This is the oldest and the largest group in Russian IR scholarship, whose development can be traced to the Soviet period. The entire Soviet theory of international relations (TIR), to a significant degree, is a product of this group's activities. Its origin lies in the early 1970s, when history of international relations was established as a relatively independent discipline and research area within studies of world history.

Within history of international relations, TIR synthesized historical analyses of specific international relations issues relying primarily on empirical observations rather than on ideological dogmas. For this reason, TIR earned the reputation of one of the most "revisionist," "liberal," and ideologically disloyal disciplines in the Soviet Union. It stood apart from other social sciences, which complied with some of the most rigid official dogmas of Marxism-Leninism. The first serious Russian forays into IR research originated at the Institute of World Economy and International Relations, under the leadership of its liberal directors, academician Nikolai N. Inozemtsev and Vladimir I. Gantman (Gantman 1976, 1984), and at the Moscow State Institute of International Relations, attached to the Ministry of Foreign Affairs, under the leadership of Mark A. Khrustalev and Anatoli A. Zlobin (Antyukhina-Moskovchenko, Zlobin, and Khrustalev 1988).

At these institutions, research was primarily conducted in the Realist spirit. It could have not been otherwise—only the Realist paradigm, with its special attention to the world's conflicts and contradictions, could co-exist somewhat peacefully with the official Soviet dogmas of class analysis in international relations. Any attempt to reject such emphasis on conflicts and contradictions would have inevitably resulted in ideologically-driven purges of the "liberally" rebellious academics. Therefore, most theorists preferred not to challenge the official paradigm directly. Rather, they developed a methodology that was somewhat compatible with official ideology. While incorporating existing works on national interest by Hans Morgentau, Morton Kaplan and Raymond Aron, they were not politically or rhetorically offensive to the Communist Party. Such logic of "self-defense" defined the approach of the majority of Russian scholars at the time.

Not surprisingly, many works in the late Soviet and post-Soviet era were influenced by the historical systemic school (Khrustalev 1990; Khrustalev, Bogaturov, and Kosolapov 2002). This school nurtured the scholarship of some leading Russian political and military theorists (Pozdnyakov 1976, 82; Arbatov 1984; Kokoshin 1989; Rogov 1989), as well as conflict theorists (Kremenyuk 1991; Kremenyuk, Sjostedt, and Zartman 1998). The first systemic and historical analysis of international relations in the XXth century (Bogaturov 2001), a four-volume collective work, was also written in this tradition.

Structuralist school

The Structuralist school represents a relatively new and politically less conservative school, which attempts to understand the modern world order in terms different from the Realist approaches dominant in the United States. This group views the world as a global entity and analyzes this entity's main laws and developmental tendencies. Structuralists emphasize various mechanisms of interaction and conflict that are characteristic of typologically different world units. They are also preoccupied with the issue of Russia's integration into the world. Originally associated with the names of Reisner and Simoniya (1984), in the last decades this school has produced new research by Cheshkov (1999), Volodin and Shirokov (2002), Bogaturov and Vinogradov (2002), and many others. There are some differences between Russian structuralists and their Western counterparts. Western IR does not seem to have anything similar to the heavily geopolitical Russian structuralist tradition. This is hardly a surprise when one considers that the West has not experienced the high-intensity geopolitical identity debates that are so characteristic of the Russian cultural tradition.

Geopolitics and geoeconomics

Geopolitics and geoeconomics have not yet established themselves as independent academic schools, and their chances of doing so in the future are not particularly hopeful. For instance, Dugin's (1998) work presents an oversimplified interpretation of the role of natural and geographic factors in international relations, an approach that is degrading to scholarly study. Fortunately, there are serious works associated with the two schools, namely those of Kolosov and Mironenko (2002), Zamyatin (2001a, b), Panarin (1995, 2002), Gadzhiyev (2000), Tsymburski (1999), and Pleshakov (1994). Geopolitics is analytically related to Western geopolitical studies.[3] Geoeconomics began to develop in Russia in the 1990s with the works of Kochetov (1997, 1999).

---

[3]   See Eduard Solovyev's essay in this issue for a more detailed analysis. Mikhail Il'yin and Stanislav Tkachenko elaborate on Structuralist and Political Economy approaches, respectively.

Political philosophy and sociology

Political philosophers and sociologists develop the macrotheoretical and sociological aspects of international relations. Political philosophy of international relations is only at the beginning of its development. It is often associated with the work by Alekseyeva (2001). In the field of sociology, important and pioneering works have been published by Pavel A. Tsygankov of Moscow State University. His works (1996, 1998, 2002) draw attention to the methodological potential of general sociology for understanding international relations. An especially important publication on this subject is his edited volume *International Relations: Sociological Approaches* (Tsygankov 1998). Like political philosophy, sociological approaches in Russian IR are also at the stage of formation. It is illustrative that out of the eleven chapters in Tsygankov's book, only four were contributed by Russian, with the rest being written by Americans and Western Europeans. Yet the accomplishments of the school are highly significant and could eventually result in a Russian school of social constructivist research.

Political psychology

Russian research in the Political Psychology tradition is heavily concentrated on conflict. The already mentioned Viktor A. Kremenyuk is an expert on conflict resolution in the historical systemic school. Marina M. Lebedeva (1998) had also studied conflicts, and is particularly attentive to behavioral and psychological characteristics of the conflict's participants, as well as to group consciousness. Feldman's (1997) and earlier works by Kosolapov (1983) can also be placed in this category.

Political economy

Finally, Political Economy of International Relations is beginning to take off in Russia. This discipline is new even in comparison to Philosophy or Sociology of International Relations. The most visible figures here are Vladislav L. Inozemtsev (1998, 1999; Il'yin and Inozemstev 2001), Yuri V. Shishkov (1997), the afore-mentioned Volodin and Shirokov (2002), and others. This discipline is represented primarily by economists who have developed an interest in political processes and who analyze power from the vantage point of the state's economic resources and its ability to exert influence over private actors.

2.2 Main issues

As we have mentioned before, the main issues discussed by the Realists are the issues of the global power structure and Russia's strategy for adjusting to this structure. The real range of issues is, of course, much broader and can be elaborated on even further. For the purpose of this essay, we will concentrate on these two since they draw most attention among Russian Realists.

World structure and polarity

While sharing some original analytical assumptions, the Realists often arrive at entirely different conclusions regarding the structure of the contemporary world. While acknowledging the obvious superiority of the United States as the world's only remaining superpower, Russian Realists interpret the situation from their own power perspective. Some scholars follow the Ministry of Foreign Affairs in its insistence upon the world's multipolar nature, or at least argue a developing trend towards multipolarity (Primakov 1996). Others view the world as unipolar in its structure. Still others propose a compromise concept of "pluralistic unipolarity" (Bogaturov 1996). According to the latter, there is only one pole in the world, but this pole has a collective nature, and it consists of the U.S. and other countries of the G-8, who are united in their ability to influence international affairs, and share a sense of responsibility for maintaining stability in the world[4]. All of these approaches are united by their understanding of the power superiority of the United States. The differences between them have to do with the political and emotional attitude toward the situation—some acknowledge victory of the strongest, others ignore it, and still others accept what they see as an objective reality while still searching for ways Russia could benefit from it.

---

[4] Below we analyze these contradictions in greater detail. The most detailed analysis of Russian Realist debates can be found in Shakleyina (2002).

The division between Structural Realists and radical Geopoliticians is instructive. The Structuralists see the processes of world development as dominated by the West, but assume that coexistence and gradual mutual adaptation of Western and non-Western societies within the global system is possible. They insist that the choice to adapt is a necessary choice for non-Western societies and Russia, although they do emphasize the importance of preserving their cultural and civilizational differences (Il'yin and Inozemtsev 2001). The structuralists view globalization as an irrevocable global trend, over which the U.S. can exert influence through competitive advantage, but cannot be controlled. On the other hand, Geopoliticians directly link global trends to the West's, specifically the United States' intentions to destroy the coherence and territorial integrity of Russia. In support of their argument, Geopoliticians often cite the work by Brzezinski (1998), in which such intentions can indeed be easily found. They see globalization, with its potential to undermine the nation–state, merely as an instrument the West is using in its struggle to eliminate Russia, China and, perhaps India as powerful geopolitical competitors (Baburin 1998).

Strategy and foreign policy

The largest divergence of opinions exists with regard to the issue of Russia's strategy and foreign policy. Realists agree that foreign policy strategy must be based upon national interests and on the state's firmness in defending Russia's national interests in relations with the outside world. The majority of the Realists also do not trust the U.S., pointing to multiple examples of unilateralism, arrogance even towards its allies, disregard for international organizations, and excessive reliance on the use of force.

The Realists disagree, however, on the appropriate foreign policy orientation for Russia. At least three distinct positions can be identified. Some Realists, represented in the influential Council on Foreign and Defence Policy, are in favor of concentrating on the former Soviet area, citing Russia's limited foreign policy resources and the need to solve a number of pressing internal problems (Pleshakov 1994; Tsymburski 1994). Others find the answer to global challenges in a creation of a Russia-China axis against the U.S. or establishing geoeconomic cooperation by developing relations with Asia. China and Japan are cited as successful examples of such a strategy (Anisimov 1994; Kochetov 1997, 1999; Baburin 1998). Still others (Kremenyuk 2001; Bogaturov 2002; Rogov 2002) support an alliance with Western countries, which would include relationships with both the U.S. and Western Europe, but only on conditions acceptable to Russia.

In part, these disagreements among Russian Realists can be attributed to their diverse perceptions of the external threat. Some associate the main threat with the U.S. global hegemonic ambitions and its efforts to turn the world into an American sphere of influence. Such efforts and ambitions, they argue, increase pressures upon the existing fragile world order and do not leave any room for self-regulating and natural mechanisms of international relations to play their critical role and reduce the world's escalating tension. Others, however, do not relate Russia's main threats to the activities of the U.S. In their view, Russia must cooperate with the United States and other countries in addressing more serious threats, such as controlling nuclear and conventional proliferation, terrorism, and drug-trafficking. This group faults the U.S. not for its hegemonic foreign policy, but rather for the inadequate attention it gives to Moscow's similar interests in addressing these threats. Below, we elaborate on these disagreements.

3. Realist debates after the Soviet collapse

World order

Bogaturov (1996a) provides a working definition of world order, by which he means a system of international relations that is regulated by

(1)   a set of principles for foreign policy behavior;

(2)   specific norms negotiated upon those principles;

(3)   accepted moral rules and sanctions for their violation;

(4)   sufficient material potential of powerful countries and institutions responsible for the implementation of sanctions;

(5)   political will of the main countries-participants to use that potential.

Immediately after the collapse of the USSR, the problem of world order receded from the center of foreign policy discussions. Geopolitical confusion prevailed. Russia was preoccupied with its internal political and economic problems, and it saw the solution in attempting to integrate into the world of developed Western countries. Nevertheless, some representatives of the Realist school continued to draw attention to the problem of international order, arguing that the emerging world would be multipolar and that an interaction of all great powers, including Russia, would be instrumental in defining the trajectory of world development. At the same time, the proclaimed return of the international system to the state of multipolarity caused concern. For instance, Sergei Rogov (1992) wrote about the danger of a "new world disorder," arguing that a long-term stability was very hard to achieve in a multipolar world. The authoritative theorist El'giz A. Pozdnyakov (1992) compared the change in the structure of international relations to a global catastrophe and warned about the serious potential of disintegration for Russia and Europe.

Bogaturov (1993) was also among those working on to the problem of world order and the potential of world destabilization. In his argument, the world was going though a transition where some elements of the old bipolar system co-existed with the newly-emerged special role of the U.S. in the international system. In Bogaturov's view, the world was going through a crisis of its systemic regulation, the deepest one since the World War II. The Russian scholar argued that the destruction of the Cold War order could not mean an automatic return to unipolarity if multipolarity was to be understood as the traditional balance of power that existed among great European powers during the 19th century. Bogaturov reasoned that bipolarity was associated with a significant gap in capabilities between the two superpowers and the rest of the world, and unipolarity with overwhelming superiority of one over all others. Then the transitional world structure after 1991 should have been defined as "one and a half-polarity," in which there were still two main poles with one (American) significantly exceeding the other (Bogaturov 1996b, 26, 30-32, 36).

Without rejecting the thinking in terms of poles and capabilities, Bogaturov therefore attempted to bridge the concepts of unipolarity and multipolarity. He also agreed that multipolarity had proven to be historically unreliable and that the world should therefore seriously entertain an alternative unipolar way of managing international conditions. In his view, the unipolar alternative could not last long—within a foreseeable future. Several powers would emerge to challenge the unipolar principles, with Russia among them. Until then, the world order should be defined as "pluralistic unipolarity" or the "unipolarity of a moderate type." Bogaturov saw Russia's key objective during this transition as avoiding challenging the unipolarity and even trying to contribute to its full-fledged stabilization. At the same time, Russia should encourage trends toward pluralization and away from unipolarity within the system (1996b, 35-36).

At this stage, the concept of a multipolar world had already become part of the official strategy of the Ministry of Foreign Affairs, but it was still far from being fully accepted by the Russian academic community. The academic Liberals rejected the concept as nonsense, whereas Realists remained divided on that issue. With Bogaturov, at least some (Kazennov and Kumachev 1997) acknowledged the benefits of unipolarity for Russia, arguing that multipolarity could in fact mean a strengthening of China and Turkey at Russia's expense. Rather than pushing for multipolarity, it was recommended that Russia concentrates its resources and solves its domestic problems.

Russia's strategy

In the early 1990s, many IR scholars and politicians favored Russia's pro-American foreign policy, thereby accepting the argument of the benefits unipolarity could bring. At the time, little effort was made to define Russia's status and national interests in the global context. Foreign policy officials were not using the Realist concepts of "great power" (*velikoderzhavnost*), "concert," and "balance of power." The above-mentioned articles by Pozdnyakov and Rogov, which used the categories and national interest concepts of geopolitics, were the exception, not the rule. The very choice of strategy was conducted under the conditions of disarray and the destruction of established institutions, theories, approaches, and foreign policy mechanisms.[5]

However, even at this period the Realists were able to make an important contribution to Russia's understanding of its role and strategy in the world. They worked hard to convince the authorities and the public that Russia's national interests and political values of the Russian Federation were not the same and had to be differentiated both in theory and in practical policy. One critic of the 1992-1993 policy course wrote the following:

> For some time, ideas have became a goal in itself, replacing geopolitical interests. The point, however, is to find a reasonable balance between liberal and pluralistic ideas on the one hand and the relatively constant geopolitically-determined interests that address the conditions of a country's survival and stability as a national and state entity on the other (Bogaturov 1994, 34).

The Realists also pointed out that the global period of Russia's foreign policy had ended, and a new, continental one had begun, an inevitable outcome given the country's more limited resources and its lessened ability to use the resources effectively under the conditions of a national crisis. In this situation, Russia was recommended to focus on its regional priorities and to rethink its prestige and influence in pragmatic and economic terms (Bogaturov 1994, 49-50). Russia was not going to automatically lose its status as an international key player with Soviet disintegration because it would continue to have:

(1)   a stabilizing capability within Eurasia (first of all, on the territory of the former USSR), and, therefore, globally;

(2)   the geopolitical function of bridging the uniting and prosperous Europe, and the poor and divided Asia.

The Realists (Bogaturov, Kozhokin, and Pleshakov 1992, 13) argued that it was thanks to the geopolitical capabilities of Russia that the Soviet Union—although under the entirely different ideological paradigm—had been able to fulfill these three paramount functions in world politics.

---

5   In Alexei G. Arbatov's (1994) description, Russia's foreign policy at that time lacked support or even interaction with parliament. Nor did it have considerable support among the public, political parties, media, and public organizations. The officials held absolutely no interest in independent foreign policy analysis, and the connection with the academic community was non-existent.

4. Contemporary Realism and its prominence

World order

In the second half of the 1990s, U.S. global strategy had became clearer, and American international actions began to look as increasingly contradictory to its claims of democratic world leadership. In Russia, the government committed itself to the concept of a multipolar world, as evidenced by publications of Primakov (1996), the Russia's Minister of Foreign Affairs as of January 1996. Russian scholars had not come to agreement concerning the characteristics of post-bipolar international system, which refreshed the debate on world order, strengthening the position of critics of unipolarity and broadening the circle of participants.

The authoritative philosopher and political scientist Batalov (2001) coined the definition of contemporary world order as "polarless" and suggested viewing the poles as powerful subsystems that form the extreme points of the global axis and hold the world system together. In Batalov's interpretation, the poles represent different civilizations that have different social, political and economic systems, as well as different ideational and value orientations. The poles are symmetrical in their power and potential for action and are able to balance each other. They simultaneously perform the roles of guarantors of the world order stability and of legislators of political game rules, which must be followed by all, or almost all, actors in the political arena. They are dependent on each other to support the internal and external status-quo, and yet they try to eliminate each other as competitors. The disappearance of one pole means an automatic collapse of the other, and with it, the collapse of the whole old world system.

This is exactly what happened in the late 1980-the early 1990s. Batalov's criticism of the multipolarity theory was that it misrepresented what the poles were and that it was an impossible approach to implement, since a system with poles can only be bipolar and nothing else. In this scholar's view, the current situation of "polarlessness" is temporary, and it does not exclude the existence of various patterns of interaction and confrontation among powerful actors in the world. This situation is, however, fundamentally unstable and, although it might sound like an exaggeration, it deserves the name of "global disorder."

Political scientist Yakovlev (2000) wrote about the emergence of a new bipolar system, though with a more complicated polarity than in the previous system. In his view, the ideologically-divided bipolar system has been replaced by a system in which only one pole—the West—is relatively stable and united. The rest of the world remains rather unstable. It consists of autonomous units which lack a clear, well-articulated understanding of their goals and priorities. In Yakovlev's view, it is this lack of understanding that explains why some of these units, such as Russia, China, and India, do not cooperate enough with each other, despite the obvious possibility of gaining greater global influence through cooperation.

According to Yakovlev, the military intervention in Yugoslavia in the spring of 1999 demonstrated the failure of the multipolar world system to provide global peace and stability. The common position of the United States and other Western countries toward the former Yugoslavia, as well as toward Russia's war in Chechnya, and the development of the Ballistic Missile Defense Treaty demonstrated that the West did exist and act as a united pole. It is for that reason that the West has been able to impose itself on others and to get away with its promotion of Western democratic and liberal ideals, even by means of military intervention. In Yakovlev's view, there are two possible scenarios for future development: either the West will use its power potential to rule the world unilaterally, or the non-Western "periphery" will manage to unite and act cohesively in order to make itself heard, thereby prolonging the era of bipolarity.

Kosolapov (1999) does not challenge the idea of bipolarity, but characterizes the essence and evolution of the international system in a different way. He defines the contemporary system of international relations as "post-Soviet," in which the West undoubtedly dominates, and authoritarian ways of regulating world order are becoming increasingly common. Kosolapov cites the strengthening of NATO and the United States at the expense of international law, the United Nations, and the Security Council as evidence of the increasing authoritarianism of the "post-Soviet system." In this scholar's view, such "two-dimensional" relations between the world's "center" and "periphery" would gradually evolve into a different, "three-dimensional" and more pluralistic type of relationship. In Kosolapov's view, this is likely to occur with the development of globalization processes, during the period from 2012 to 2025 serving as the critical one in moving beyond the "post-Soviet" world order.

Russia's strategy

In 1994, Russia's leadership adopted the pragmatic way of thinking that had been advocated by the Realist academic and political community and defined the country's geostrategic priorities in terms of national interests. With this began the process of consolidation of Russia, a process that required the development of a national ideology and the emergence of more nationally-oriented policies. All major political parties and movements supported the new agenda of reviving Russia as a great power. The idea of "enlightened patriotism" occupied central place in the new great-power ideology.[6] Kortunov (1995) introduced the concept of "enlightened democratic patriotism" and defined it as the "ideology of Russian revival, which combines the idea of individual freedom in an open society with the idea of strong and responsible state power." The notions of enlightened patriotism and realism, formulated by Russian strategists in 1995-1996, informed Russia's new Foreign Policy Doctrine, the document which made official the country's geopolitical priorities and principal policy directions. At about the same time, there was a visible intensification of foreign policy discussions and a heightened level of criticism directed at the Foreign Ministry and its Minister, Andrei V. Kozyrev.

In 1996, Primakov was appointed as the new Foreign Minister, which facilitated the adoption of the multipolar world concept as the baseline of Russia's new foreign policy. Primakov initiated an active bilateral dialogue with U.S. and NATO and activated Russia's regional policies in the Middle East and Asia. He also announced Russia's new commitment to building close relations with the Soviet successor states and made progress in establishing an alliance between Russia and Belarus. The new Minister embraced multipolarity as the

---

[6] In 1992, the very word "patriot" was part of vocabulary for only the radical nationalist and communist opposition.

desired foreign policy goal and defined the new era as one of transition from confrontational to democratic principles in international relations (1996). During this transition, he argued, different power centers, including Russia, would play a considerable role.

Another prominent characteristic of this period has been a rising interest to non-Western parts of the world. Several political scientists, such as Tsymburski (1994), Bogaturov (1996a), and Larin (1997), argued that the fixation of Russian IR community on unipolarity and the role of the United States was unwarranted and that it shifted intellectual resources away from other key issues, such as the future of Siberia and the Far East.[7] It was their belief that with China's rapid development the Russian Far East was increasingly becoming an area of China's geoeconomic and cultural influence.

The renewal of interest to the non-Western world did not mean a loss of the Realists' interest in the United States or the West in general. It simply meant, in Krivokhizha's (2001) view, that Russia's international activities had to include both global and regional dimensions, and that active policy in one direction was not an indicator of declining attention to other directions. In Rogov's (1996) formulation:

> Under the conditions of continuous economic crisis and the collapsing industry, one of [Russia's] most important objectives is to prevent the consolidation of a new system of international relations, in which Russia would be left in isolation ... Besides seeking friends in the South and the East [Russia must] prevent confrontation with the West. The return to a Cold War era would be lethal for us.

5. The future of Realism and the question of Russia's state identity

The position of the majority of Russian Realists is one of pragmatism, and it is principally different from both the views of Liberals and of Realists of extreme orientation. At the core of these differences lies the question of the very identity of the new Russian state. In Kortunov's (1997, 5-7) formulation, "the crisis

---

[7] Tsymburski (1994) articulated this concern earlier than others.

of identity is the main crisis that Russia has been experiencing after the dissolution of the USSR."

Andrei Mel'vil's (1998) position is illustrative of Russian liberal views. In his
argument, Russia's main objective should be the completion of internal
reforms rather than the pursuit of international activities:

> At present, Russia's priorities are internal. It is our historical
> chance to solve the long- postponed problems of Russia's
> well-being, its people, and society. Our present historical
> "challenge" is internal modernization, the construction of a
> democratic political system, and a structural transformation
> of the economy and the social sphere, not a state-controlled
> oligarchical regime dreaming of the country's past geopoliti-
> cal power ... [the transition should be] from the construction
> of a liberal-democratic and prosperous society to the rees-
> tablishment of new place in the world" (Mel'vil' 1998, 84-85).

In Mel'vil's opinion, an active foreign policy can only be justified if it has in mind
internal problems and aids in their solution. To him, Russia's new identity must
be associated with its democratic and post-imperial transformation.

Dugin's (1998) position is just the opposite, and his emphasis is upon the
unique historical territory of the Russian state, its civilizational mission, political
integrity, and economic self-sufficiency. According to this position, the status of
a "regional state," which has been imposed on Russia by the West, can only
be compared to geopolitical suicide of Russia and of its principally imperial
identity (1998, 193). To Dugin and others, the loss of the Soviet empire is a
tragedy of catastrophic proportion. It means the end of Russia's participation in
the world and the collapse of its spiritual and cultural system of values, one
which inspired so many generations of Russians to heroism, victory, struggle,
and overcoming of difficulties (Dugin 1998, 193-213). One cannot accept the
views of Dugin's supporters without reservation. At the same time, one cannot
ignore the fact that the U.S. has written off the nation-state as the main ele-
ment of the international system, and that it no longer views national sovereignty and state boundaries as an obstacle for intervention when regional and
international security is at stake. Despite this view, the world is not homogeneous, and the principle of national sovereignty remains a priority for many

states, including Russia, who do not want to become an object of "humanitarian intervention" led by NATO or anybody else. Russia is not ready to play the role of a junior partner and follow in the lockstep of the United States.

The Realists believe that Russian identity should be associated with the historical tradition of a great power. For example, in Batalov's (2000) view, "*velikoderzhavnost*" (commitment to great power status) is at the heart of the culture and psyche of Russia. This cultural archetype will continue to shape Russian perceptions of international events, regardless of its internal conditions. Russia remains and will remain a great power. It possesses this status because of a whole complex of unchanged considerations: its geopolitical position, substantial military and nuclear capabilities, the tremendous reserves of its natural resources, the unique intellectual and spiritual potentials, and its demography. The integral criterion of the country's great statehood is in its ability to influence world affairs in a profound way, as well as in the inability of the world community to ignore Russia's strategic interests (Batalov 2000, 33-37). Yet, Russia's historical continuity and uniqueness is compatible with reform priorities and does not imply either its failure, as Dugin argues, or its confrontation with the rest of the world, as Mel'vil' and other liberals assume.

Although the "Russian Idea" and the "American Dream" do not provide a solid ground for a stable friendship between the two countries, they also do not encourage hostility that could lead to mutual destruction. If the United States and the West in general are unwilling to understand Russia's difference and continue to view the "Russian Idea" as that of nationalism or imperialism, then there are likely to be more errors in Western policies toward Russia. America needs Russia as a partner in finding solutions to global and regional problems. Russia also needs America. Many in Russia acknowledge the fact that the U.S. remains the most formidable military power and that without cooperation with the U.S., Russia will have no guarantee of national security. In addition, there are few Russians who don't understand the critical role the U.S. plays in the financial and economic development of their country.

Therefore, one can conclude that Russia will have to address both its internal and its external tasks. It must successfully conduct reforms, and must maintain its international status by carrying out active foreign policies in the Eastern and Western directions. Actions in the internal and external area are closely interrelated, and the success in one will inevitably strengthen the chances of success in another. It seems that a social and intellectual consensus along these lines is gradually being formed in Russia. The issue at stake is which Russia will be favored by the leadership and the society. Would Russians be willing to sacrifice to achieve the status of a great power, or would they ultimately be satisfied with the rank of an ordinary but well-off country?

References

Alekseeva, T. A. 2001. Sovremennye politicheskie teorii. ROSSPEN, Moskva.

Anisimov, A. 1994. Mirovoi konfliktny potentsial i Rossiya. Rossia XXI 1-2.

Antyukhina-Moskovchenko, V. I., A. A. Zlobin, M. A. Khroustalev. 1988. Osnovy teorii mezhdunarodnykh otnosheniy. MGIMO, Moskva.

Arbatov, A. G. 1984. Voenno-strategicheskiy paritet i politika Soedinennykh Shtatov Ameriki. Politizdat, Moskva.

Arbatov, A. G. 1994. Interesy Rossii v SNG. Mezhdunarodnaya zhizn' 9.

Baburin, S. N. 1998. Mirovoi poryadok posle Sovetskogo Soyuza i territorialnyi vopros. Natsyonal'nye interesy 1.

Batalov, E. Ya. 2000. Russkaya ideya i Amerikanskaya mechta. SShA i Kanada: ekonomika, politika, kultura 11.

Batalov, E. Ya. 2001. Novaya epokha—novy mir. Svobodnaya mysl' 1.

Bogaturov, A. D., ed. 1994. Etap za globalnym. Liberalny natsionalizm vo vneshnei politike Rossiyi. Institut SShA i Kanady, Moskva.

Bogaturov, A. D., M. M. Kozhokin, and K. V. Pleshakov. 1992. Posle imperii: demokratizm i derzhavnost vo vneshnei politike Rossii. Institut SShA i Kanady, Moskva.

Bogaturov, A. D. 1993. Krizis mirosistemnogo regulirovaniya. Mezhdunarodnaya zhizn' 7.

Bogaturov, A. D. 1996a. Velikiye derzhavy na Tikhom okeane. Nauka, Moskva.

Bogaturov, A. D. 1996b. Plyuralisticheskaya odnopolyarnost' i interesy Rossii. Svobodnaya mysl' 2.

Bogaturov, A. D., ed. 2001. Sistemnaya istoriya mezhdunarodnykh otnosheniy. Vol. 1-2. Moskovskiy rabochiy, Moskva.

NEW DIRECTIONS IN RUSSIAN INTERNATIONAL STUDIES 79

Bogaturov, A. D. 2002. Alyans nesoglasnykh. Nezavisimaya gazeta, 22 November.

Bogaturov, A. D., A. V. Vinogradov. 2002. Anklavno-konglomerativny tip razvitiya. In: Vostok-Zapad-Rossiya. Progress-Traditsiya, Moskva.

Brzezinski, Z. 1998. Velikaya shakhmatnaya doska. Progress, Moskva.

Cheshkov, M. A. 1999. Globalny Kontext postsovetskoi Rossii, MONF, Moskva.

Davydov, Yu. P. 2002. Norma protiv sily. Institut SShA i Kanady, Moskva.

Dugin, A. 1998. Osnovy geopolitiki. Arktogeya, Moskva.

Feldman, D. M. 1997. Konflikty v mirovoi politike. Bratya Karich, Moskva.

Gadzhiev, K. S. 2000. Geopolitika. Yuniti, Moskva.

Gantman, V. I., ed. 1976. Sovremennyye burzhuaznyye teorii mezhdunarodnykh otnosheniy. Nauka, Moskva.

Gantman, V. I., ed. 1984. Systema, struktura i protses razvitiya sovremennykh mezhdunarodnykh otnosheniy. Nauka, Moskva.

Il'yin, M. V. and V. L. Inozemtsev, eds. 2001. Megatrendy mirovogo razvitiya. Tsentr issledovaniya postindustrial'nogo obshchestva, Moskva.

Inozemtsev, V. L. 1998. Za predelami ekonomicheskogo obshchestva. Akademiya, Moskva.

Inozemtsev, V. L. 1999. Raskolotaya tsivilizatsiya. Akcademiya-Nauka, Moskva.

Kazennov, S. and V. Kumachev. 1997. Epokha razrusheniya bipolyarnogo mirustroistva. NG-stsenariyi 8.

Khrustalev, M. A. 1990. Teoriya politiki i politicheskiy analiz. MGIMO, Moskva.

Khrustalev, M. A., A. D. Bogaturov, N. A. Kosolapov. 2002. Ocherki teorii i politicheskogo analiza mezhdunarodnykh otnosheniy. Nauchno-obrazovatel'ny forum po mezhdunarodnym otnosheniyam, Moskva.

Kochetov, E. 1997. Geoekonomika i strategiya Rossii. Ekonomika, Moskva.

Kochetov, E. 1999. Geoekonomika. Ekonomika, Moskva.

Kokoshin, A. A. 1989. V poiskakh vykhoda: voenno-politicheskiye aspekty mezhdunarodnoi bezopasnosti. Politizdat, Moskva.

Kolosov, V.A. and N.S. Mironenko. 2002. Geopolitika i politicheskaya geografiya. Aspekt-press, Moskva.

Kortunov, S. V. 1995. Natsional'naya sverkhzadacha. Opyt rossiyskoi ideologuii. Nezavisimaya gazeta, 7 October.

Kortunov, S. V. 1997. Rossiya: natsionalnaya identichnost' na rubezhe vekov. MONF, Moskva.

Kosolapov, N. A. 1983. Politicheskaya psikhologiya i mezhdunarodnye otnosheniya. Nauka, Moskva.

Kosolapov, N. A. 1999. Kontury novogo miroporyadka. In: Postindustrial'ny mir: tsentr, peripheriya, Rossiya. IMEMO, Moskva.

Kremenyuk, V., ed. 1991. International Negotiations: Analysis, Approaches, Issues. Jossey Bass, San Francisco.

Kremenyuk, V. 2001. Soedinennye Shtaty Ameriki i okruzhayushiy mir. SShA i Kanada: ekonomika, politika, cultura 1.

Krivokhizha, V. 2001. Vneshnyaya politika Rossii i izmeneniye sistemnosti mezhdunarodnykh otnosheniy. Mezhdunarodnaya zhizn' 4.

Larin, P. L. 1997. Rossiya i Kitai na poroge tret'ego tysyachiletiya. Problemy Dal'nego Vostoka 1.

Lebedeva, M. M. 1998. Politicheskoye uregulirovaniye konfliktov. Gardarika, Moskva.

Mel'vil', A. Yu. 1998. Liberal'naya vneshnepoliticheskaya alternative dlya Rossii. Otkrytaya politika 6.

Panarin, A. S. 1995. Evraziysky proyekt v mirosistemnom kontekste. Vostok 2.

Panarin, A. S. 2002. Iskusheniye globalizmom. Algoritm, Moskva.

Pleshakov, K. V. 1994. Geo-ideologicheskaya paradigma. No publisher information, Moskva.

Pozdnyakov, E. A. 1976. Sistemnyi podkhod i mezhdunarodnyye otnosheniya. Nauka, Moskva.

Pozdnyakov, E. A. 1992. Geopoliticheksy kollaps i Rossiya. Mezhdunarodnaya zhizn' 8-9.

Primakov, E. M. 1996. Mezhdunarodnye otnosheniya nakanune XXI veka. Mezhdunarodnaya zhizn' 10.

Reisner, L. I. and N. A. Simonia, eds. 1984. Evolyutsiya vostochnykh obshchestv. Nauka, Moskva.

Rogov, S. M. 1989. Sovetskiy Soyuz i Soedinennye Shtaty Ameriki: poisk balansa interesov. Mezhdunarodnye otnosheniya, Moskva.

Rogov, S. M. 1992. Rossiya i Soedinennye Shtaty Ameriki v mnogopolyarnom mire. SShA: ekonomika, politika, ideologiya 10.

Rogov, S. M. 1996. Nas vytalkivayut iz Evropy. Vek, 25-31 October.

Rogov, S. M. 2002. Doktrina Busha i perspektivy rossiysko-amerikanskikh otnosheniy. Nezavisimaya gazeta, 3 April.

Shishkov, Y. V., ed. 1997. Blizhnee i dalnee zarubezhie v geoekonomicheskoi strategiyi Rossii. IMEMO, Moskva.

Shakleyina, T. A. 2002. Rossia i Soedinennye Shtaty Ameriki v novom mirovom poryadke. Institut Soedinennykh Shtatov Ameriki i Kanady, Moskva.

Tsygankov, P. A. 1996. Mezhdunarodnye otnosheniya. Vysshaya shkola, Moskva.

Tsygankov, P. A., ed. 1998. Mezhdunarodnye otnosheniya: sotsiologicheskiye podkhody. Gardarika, Moskva.

Tsygankov, P. A. 2002. Teoriya mezhdunarodnykh otnosheniy. Gardarika, Moskva.

Tsymburski, V. L. 1994. Natsyonalnye interesy Rossii. Vestnik Moskovskogo universiteta: Sotsialno-politicheskiye issledovaniya 3.

Tsymburski, V. L. 1999. Geopolitika dlya "yevraziyskoi Atlantidy." Pro et Contra 4 (4)

Volodin, A.G. and G. K. Shirokov. 2002. Globalizatsiya. Institut Vostokovedeniya RAN, Moskva.

Yakovlev, A. G. 2000. I vse zhe na gorizonte dvukhpolyusny mir. Problemy Dal'nego Vostoka 4.

Zamyatin, D. N. 2001a. Geopolitika: osnovnye problemy i itogi razvitiya v XX veke. Polis 6.

Zamyatin, D. N. 2001b. Geograficheskiye obrazy mirovogo razvitiya. Obshchestvennye nauki i sovremennost' 1.

IV. Dilemmas and promises of Russian Liberalism

Pavel A. Tsygankov and Andrei P. Tsygankov

1. Introduction: Russian Liberal IR between Western ideas and national democracy

Russian Liberalism has accumulated considerable experience and traditions. It has progressed historically in polemics with supporters of the strong state, and in its external orientations it gravitates toward the West. The disintegration of USSR sharpened many of the traditional Liberal disputes by placing them in a new context. Contemporary Liberals develop their argumentations in polemics with Statists and National Communists, who defend the values of the strong state and Russia's civilizational uniqueness and who view the world in terms of a struggle for power and resources.[1] The present essay analyzes the divisions within Russian Liberals and the contradictory nature of this intellectual movement.

Typically, Liberals are associated with the values of freedom, tolerance and democracy in the world. Liberalism, however, may be shaped differently in different social and cultural contexts. If it is valid to pose the question of national models of socialism, as it has been customary in Russia (Kiselev and Klyamkin 1989), than it may be no less important to view liberalism as nationally distinct. Russian Liberalism is different from Western, Chinese, Arab or others, and such cultural specifics should become an important premise for understanding its nature.

There exist deep divisions and disagreements among Russian liberals. This intellectual movement often includes people with rather differing political orientations. To so-called Westernizers continue to enjoy hegemonic position within the movement. This group acknowledges Russia's differences from the West, but associates such differences with the former's backwardness. Westernizers

---

[1] For various attempts to categorize Russian foreign policy schools, see Light 1996; Tsygankov 1997; Shlapentokh 1998; Sergunin 2000; Tsygankov 2001, 2003.

believe in the existence of the single path of mankind's development, unequivocally associating this path with the West and viewing Western politico-economic institutions as the example for Russia and the rest of the world to follow. This thinking can be traced back to Milyukov's (1992) "Essays on Russian culture" or even earlier. In today's Russia, it has been actively defended through the intellectual and political efforts of the early reformers, such as Andrei Kozyrev and Yegor Gaydar, and those of the current theoreticians of such political parties as the Union of the Right Wing Forces and Yabloko. The Westernizers themselves are not united. Although they all insist that Russia must borrow from the West, they disagree on the question of which West to follow. Some see the United States as the ultimate model, while others associate Russia's progress with borrowing from the experiences of Germany, and Northern or Eastern Europe.

In addition, there has always existed a distinct school of thought in Russia critical of the Westernizers' philosophy, which has argued the necessity for Russia to mobilize its own experience of democratic transformation. The National Democratic school is not as influential, nor does it have very prominent politicians to embrace its message. This can partly be explained by the political failure of Gorbachev's ideas, some of which were close to the National Democratic philosophy. Nevertheless, this philosophy deserves serious attention and will be analyzed in greater details in this paper.

The issues most often debated by Russian liberals can be grouped in three categories of questions: Which world order is emerging after the Cold War and which one is the most preferable for Russia? How are the state, its sovereignty, and national interests affected in the new era of globalization? What kind of foreign policy strategy should Russia adopt to adequately respond the new world's challenges and conditions? These are the questions that are not only being continuously debated by the Liberals, Realists, and representatives of other IR theories, but also within Liberals themselves. These debates have undergone two distinct stages: from the disintegration of the USSR to the mid-1990s, and from the mid-1990s to the present. The September 11, 2001 terrorist attacks against the United States have once again changed the context in which these debates progress.

The above described disagreements within Russian liberals can be understood in terms of the familiar debate between supporters of cosmopolitan and communitarian thought. Cosmopolitans insist on the emergence of a single humanity and emphasize the factors of a unifying and homogenizing nature. Russian Modernizers have a deterministic worldview and see the world as persistently adapting to the institutions of the market economy created in the West a long time ago. Another liberal school—Liberal Institutionalists—also point to the growing homogeneity in the world, but link it to the activity and improvement of existing global and international institutions. As for the National Democrats, this group—in the spirit of commutarianism—underscores the role of national and cultural foundations in building democratic institutions. Without denying the significance of the West and international institutions in this process, the National Democrats insist that such a country as Russia cannot be reformed from the outside and must find and mobilize national experience to achieve this goal.

2. The Soviet breakup and the schools of Russian Liberalism

The origins of Russian Liberalism can be traced back to Gorbachev's Perestroika and New Thinking, and—even to a greater extent—to the "Democratic Russia" movement and politicians like Egor Gaydar and Andrei Kozyrev, who held key governmental offices in the early stages of the post-communist transformation. Following the break-up of the Soviet Union, Russia has been witnessing the development of at least three significant schools in Liberal thinking—Modernizers, Institutionalists, and National Democrats. Their views of the Soviet Union's disappearance from the world political map differ from those of Realists, who consider that event as a geopolitical catastrophe and a potential threat to stability in Russia and the rest of the world. Yet each of those three schools has it own vision of a desirable world order and Russia's participation in it.

Modernizers

Politically, the Westernizers-Modernizers seem to be the most influential among Russian liberals. The possibility of another, non-Western type of Liberalism is not something that Westernizers are willing to accept. They are also convinced that during the Cold War Russia acted against its own national interests, which lie in integration with the West, and now Russia has to do everything in its power to achieve that goal. The school sees the West as the only progressive civilization in the world. The main threats to Russia's "genuine" identity therefore are related to its own political and economic backwardness, as well to its association with non-democratic nations, such as the former allies of the USSR. Only through integration into the community of the "Western civilized nations" can Russia adequately respond to these threats (Kozyrev 1995; Gaidar 1997).

Modernizers are perfectly convinced that all the alternatives to the West are flawed, and that the end of the Cold War signifies the victory of the Western civilization in all respects—military, economic, political, and cultural. They perceive the Soviet collapse as a positive phenomenon, which brought the elimination of threats to Russia's security and gave it the chance to adopt the "universal" values of the "civilized" world, such as the values of democracy, market economy, and protection of human rights. It is this commitment to universal values that should allow Russia "to return to the normal cycle of development, from which it fell out in the last 70 years" (Kozyrev 1992, 92). The break-up of the Soviet Union meant the end of the Cold War and an elimination of foreign threats to Russia.

In the West, Francis Fukuyama expressed a very similar viewpoint in his famous "end of history" thesis. Russian Modernizers often fully subscribe to Fukuyama's ideas.[2] In this linear perspective, Russia has no alternative to integration into the Western community, and such modernization-Westernization must take place regardless of whether anybody in Russia likes it. If Russia itself does not decisively move in this direction, modernization will come anyway—only at a much heavier social and economic price.

The early Westerners like Kozyrev and Gaydar actively promoted these views and seriously believed that Russia would become a part of the West almost immediately after it declares its loyalty to the values of Western civilization.

---

[2] For a more detailed analysis of Russian perception of Fukuyama's thesis, see Tsygankov 2004.

Institutionalists

If for Modernizers the key determining factor in Russia's success is modernization, then Institutionalists view its progress in terms of the acquisition and strengthening of membership in principal contemporary international institutions. At the same time, many Institutionalists can be quite critical of the existing institutional arrangements, and often promote various projects aimed at their improvement. This group advocates an increased role for international institutions in facilitating Russia's social and political development. Unlike Modernizers, Institutionalists are often critical of the dissolution of the USSR and refuse to view it as a definitively positive and encouraging development. Instead, Institutionalists advocate the strengthening of political and economic integration among the newly independent states in the former Soviet region. They also argue against applying categories of "victory" and "defeat" for evaluating the result of the Cold War.[3]

One can identify two competing schools within Institutionalism. The first school considers the institution of sovereign statehood as increasingly obsolete, emphasizing instead the growing role of transnational ties and global civil society. Some of Gorbachev's supporters hypothesized the emergence of a global civil society gradually producing the "conditions necessary for the establishment of a new democratic world order, which would function based on network principles rather than those of hierarchy." [4]

The second school is more moderate in its assessment of the state role and does not agree that statehood, sovereignty, or national interests have lost their significance. While emphasizing the growing role of international institutions in the world, moderate Institutionalists argue that the nation-state merely reformulates its roles and functions and does not disappear from the scene. While accepting the leading role of the West in the world, this group puts the emphasis on the importance of strengthening such institutions as the United Nations and on the necessity for Russia to seek solutions to its problems by participating in such institutions (Davydov 2002). Institutionalists are not as optimistic or

---

[3] Many liberals have been critical of the Soviet collapse. See, for example, Furman, 1992.
[4] Krasin 1996, 12. For a development of this line of thinking, see: Kapustin 1996, 14-15; Shakhnazarov 1998, 82; Gorbachev 2003.

deterministic about Russia's future, and they insist that Russia must undertake a great deal of efforts to move in the outlined direction.[5]

The roots of Russian Institutionalism may be found in the earlier efforts to improve the international system of arms control and in Gorbachev's attempts to establish a principally new political foundation for world order. In the West, the difference between radical and moderate Institutionalists can be more or less captured by comparing the stances of those theorists arguing for a radical renovation of the world's institutional structure, such as Andrew Linklater (1998), and those more sympathetic to the "international society" approach (Bull and Watson 1984) in Europe and the U.S.

National Democrats

National Democrats are close to moderate Institutionalists in their estimates of the Soviet collapse, but, as no other liberal school, they are keen on emphasizing the special nature of the Russian development path and the importance of local cultures in world politics. This school of thought shares with other Liberals the philosophy of global community, but it views the origins of global community in a distinct way. According to National Democrats, basic human rights should not be viewed as a product of the Western civilization alone. The supporters of the school refuse to perceive the world in terms of the dichotomy between "progressive" civilization and "developmentally delayed nations." Their picture of Russia's identity and the world in the post-Cold War era is more complex and dialectical.[6]

From the National Democratic perspective, Russia is an independent civilization, but also a part of the international society. In the emerging post-Cold War era, Russia and other major actors are redefining their roles and identities and are learning how to live in an increasingly inter-dependent yet diverse world. In this world, main threats are coming from two directions: the violation of basic human rights and the disrespect for cultural pluralism. The challenge

---

5   Thus Alexei Salmin pointed to what he saw as the "clear crisis and potential destabilization of the entire international system" and argued the necessity of establishing the world government (1994, 8, 10, 14).

6   See especially, Gadzhiev 2000.

is to establish a "unity in diversity" regime, in which different nations and cultures might be able to maintain intense dialogue and cooperation by observing certain globally acknowledged rules yet still follow their own internally developed sets of norms. In this regard, National Democrats are close to moderate Institutionalists, who continue to emphasize the persistent significance of nation-states in world politics. Yet, relative to Institutionalists, National Democrats' main emphasis is not international institutions, but rather Russia's own cultural legacy. The challenge for Russia, they believe, is not to copy the Western pattern but to find an appropriate culture-sensitive path to a world economic and security system.

Among liberals, this group was the first to realize the significance of the "national interest" category for Russia's development. Unlike Modernizers and some Institutionalists, who rejected such significance,[7] National Democrats saw the debate on national interests as assisting Russia in its painful self-determination after the communist era. They saw the role of this debate in helping Russian society identify its special features and decide which national values should be mobilized as a foundation for democratic reforms.[8] National Democrats also defended the principle of multi-vector foreign policy, promoting it with polemics with Modernizers and their "guru" Fukuyama. In this case, positions of National Democrats came close to those of moderate Statists or Realists, such as the advisor to the President Sergei Stankevich and the chair of the Supreme Council Committee on International Affairs Vladimir Lukin. In response to the Modernizers' call to choose the pro-American and pro-European foreign policy orientation (Makarenko 2000; Trenin 2001), they insisted

---

[7]   In their opinion, in contrast to the West, the category of national interests is inapplicable and even dangerous for Russia's fragile democracy, given Russia's legacy of heavy-handed authoritarianism and "strong state" (Abolin 1995, 110; Polyakov 1995, 108-109).

[8]   For example, Alexandr Galkin and Yuri Krasin, experts at the Gorbachev Foundation, proposed the following definition of national interest: "National interests include interests and needs of a particular socio-cultural community, satisfaction and defense of which is a necessary precondition for this community's existence and identification as a subject of history. National interests reflect the need for a national community to occupy the place in the world society that most adequately corresponds with its cultural and historical traditions and allows for implementation of its potential resources to the fullest extent" (As cit. in: Kortunov 1998, 78; for elaboration, see Krasin 1996).

upon the necessity for Russia to promote integration in the former USSR as well as to maintain relationships with countries of Asia.[9]

The relatively recent roots of National Democratic thinking can be traced to Gorbachev's new thinking and social-democratic beliefs. In fact, many of the current National Democrats have been and remain among Gorbachev's supporters. In this respect, they are close to some Institutionalists, yet, they are also quite critical of Gorbachev for his numerous concessions to the West. In the global intellectual discourse, similar positions were advocated by Robert Cox (1995) and others, who emphasized the importance of dialogue between cultures and civilizations in the world.[10]

3. The contemporary debates among Russian Liberals

Despite the political weakening of Westernizers following the victory of nationalists during the 1993 parliamentary elections and the official leadership's transition to a more moderate position, academic liberalism continued to develop. In the second half of the 1990s, Liberals took an active role in debating the issues of world order, national interests, and foreign policy orientations by further specifying and clarifying their positions. The power transition from a more liberal Yeltsin to a more statist Putin, as well as the September 11 terrorist attacks against the U.S., further reinvigorated these debates by placing them in yet another context.

World order

The understanding of world order[11] by Russian Liberals differs from that of their Realist opponents. As Shakleyina and Bogaturov clarify in their paper in

---

[9] For a similar perspective on Russia's foreign policy priorities, see Spasski 1992; Krasin 1996; Gadziyev 2000. In his earlier work (1995), Alexandr Panarin formulated a number of foreign policy principles of liberal Eurasianism. In his more recent work (1998, 2000), partly in response to some extreme views of Westernizers, Panarin moved closer to a more hard-line version of Eurasianism. For the distinctions among different currents of contemporary Eurasianism, see Tsygankov 2003.

[10] In Russia, there has also developed a fruitful tradition of studying cultural dialogue including in the global context (See, for example, Gefter 1991; Kapustin 1998; Gorbachev 2003).

[11] In this context, we view the "world" and "international" as interchangeable.

this volume, to Russian Realists the word order is, above all, the current state of international relations' system that is more or less stable. Realists view the principles, the parameters, and the content of the international system as shaped by its structure (defined by polarity and distribution of power) and by the existing institutional and normative mechanisms of international security (Kortunov 2002, 77-78). In other words, for Realists, world order refers to the already established system (Kortunov 2002, 93), whereas Liberals put the emphasis on aspects that relate to ways of improving and regulating world order (Davydov 2002, 34). Another important distinction of Liberal understanding of world order is the emphasis on pluralism of actors: while Realists write primarily—and often, exclusively—about international as interstate relations, Liberals point to a variety of non-state actors, movements and networks (Lebedeva 2003). Finally, Liberals do not limit themselves to arguing the transitional nature of the contemporary world order—Realists also acknowledge it—but also insist that there are some elements of progress in such transition and that democratic forces across the world must build on these elements to further improve world order.

At the same time, representatives of different schools within Liberalism offer different interpretations of the contents of the post-Cold War order. Despite the arrival of Putin to power, which many Liberals had met with suspicion, Modernizers and radical Institutionalists continue to view the international system as progressing in the direction of becoming homogeneously liberal and democratic, often referring to such system as unipolar. For example, Vladimir Kulagin (2002) writes about the emergence of the "democratic unipolarity." He points to the increased number of democratic states since the early 1990s and argues that their number exceeded that of authoritarian states. To this scholar, the described development indicates the "uniform and simultaneous nature of some key 'transnational' processes in the world politics" (Kulagin 2002, 147; Bunin 2003; Saburov 2003; Sheinis 2003). Another representative of this school thinks that "Fukuyama and Heilbroner were basically correct in arguing the 'end of history' thesis, which implies the absence of a viable alternative to Western liberalism and unipolar world order" (Shevtsova 2003). Many Modernizers view recent conflicts, such as Kosovo and Iraq, as characteristic of the contemporary world order, in which unipolarity and power prevail as principles of regulating world order. It is no accident that many of them also come close to being supportive of Western theories of humanitarian intervention and limited sovereignty.

The moderate Institutionalists and National Democrats see the movement toward democratic world order as something much more complicated. Institutionalists emphasize the necessity of developing international institutions, and their recommendations often differ from those of Modernizers. Not all of them—especially following the military interventions of NATO in Yugoslavia and the United States in Iraq—are supportive of Russia's membership in NATO. Instead, they favor improving the structure and the role of the United Nations (Adamishin 2002).[12] This group believes that the United States can only exercise its leadership in the world if it takes into consideration other states' interests and relies on the existing international institutions. America would not be able to preserve its hegemonic position and bear the heavy material burden of stabilizing the international system alone; it would have to respect the interests of other great powers, such as China, Japan, Great Britain, France, India, and partially Russia (Davydov 2002, 285, 227-228).

However, some Liberals observe the processes that could not be understood within the frameworks of democratic unipolarity or international institutional development. For instance, they point to the emergence of multiple centers of regional and cultural gravitation and suggest the theory of "alternative multipolarity" as a way to account for this development. Thus, Shevtsova (2003) writes about the possibility of "several centers of gravitation within the frames of the liberal system." Viktor Sergeyev (2001) and Nikita Zagladin (2000) are explicit in relating these centers of gravitation to regional developments. To them, such regional centers may constitute centers of power independent from the power of states and therefore may turn into alternative centers of political influence in the globalizing world. Approaching the position of National Democrats, Vladimir Pantin (2002) and Alexei Salmin (2001) speak against defining the contemporary world as either unipolar or multipolar. They argue that while on occasions the world looks as if it is unipolar, it more often

---

[12] On lessons learned by Russian Liberals and Nationalists from the Kosovo crisis, see Tsygankov 2001.

has qualities of a multipolar one—from the point of view of its multiple dimen-sions (national, transnational, sub-national, cultural, civilizational, temporal, and others).

Therefore, Liberal interpretations of the trends and processes of world regu-lation may vary. According to Modernizers, America plays the role of a regula-tor in the contemporary world, defending Russia and other states from "hooligans and marginalized elements" (Saburov 2003), Institutionalists insist upon the priority role of international organizations and legal norms (Borko 2001; Davydov 2002). It was no accident that the former and the latter dis-agreed regarding American military intervention in Iraq in March 2003 without UN approval. Furthermore, some Institutionalists underline the role of non-governmental organizations with "non-hierarchical responsibility" (Sergeyev 2001) and argue the withering of the state, whereas others come close to National Democrats in arguing that successful normative regulation of an inter-national system is impossible without the facilitating role of great powers (Davydov 2002, 224, 167).

The disagreement between Modernizers, on the one hand, and Institution-alists and National Democrats, on the other, can be illustrated by comparing their attitudes toward Putin's rapprochement with the U.S. after September 11, 2003. Modernizers backed Putin's decision to side with the United States after September 11, and they argued that the Russian alliance with the West should go beyond solving some tactical purposes and forge the development of a common identity and common cultural values (e.g., Yavlinski 2002; Kara-Murza 2002). The attitude of Institutionalists and National Democrats was a more complex and cautious one. While being supportive of Putin's decision and sympathetic toward the West, the group cautioned that the United States' unilateral use of power and the narrowly chosen pro-American model of glo-balization was one of the causes of the spread of terrorism (Buzgalin 2002). Some Social Democrats were also less inclined to view America and Europe as culturally similar and recommended that Putin explicitly side with Europe in the post-September 11 world (Fedorov 2002).

In some respects, the views of the Social Democrats corresponded with those of President Putin. Putin also downplayed military interventions as a long-term solution to the problem of terrorism. He did not commit Russian troops to the effort and instead emphasized the relevance of international law and the United Nations. He was also careful not to cast his actions in a pro-American or an anti-Islamic light and, immediately after the terrorist attack, warned against framing the policy response as a "war of civilizations" (Putin 2001). The latter is important given that some of Russia's Liberals moved closer to Fukuyama-Huntingtonian language in characterizing 9/11 as a clash between Western "civilization" and cultural "barbarianism" and proposing that Russia make a decisive "choice" between "barbarians" and "civilized nations" (Kara-Murza 2001).

National interest and sovereignty

As we have mentioned earlier, the issue of national interests has been in the center of IR and Political Science discussions in Russia since the Soviet disin-tegration. However, whereas the early discussions involved primarily internal aspects of national interest, such as relationships between the state and civil society, the more recent debate focuses on the issues of state sovereignty and territorial integrity.

Modernizers argue the erosion of national interests and believe that global-ization replaces national interests with those of a global civil society. The latter guarantees the personal rights and freedoms which are still being suppressed by the state, especially in the countries with authoritarian political regimes. The "erosion" of institutions of nation-state and sovereignty is associated by Mod-ernizers and some Institutionalists with the "development of international insti-tutions that seek to guarantee civil rights, expansion of transnational corporations, and trends toward regional integration" (Sergeyev 1999, 28). Some are willing to go as far as to deny the significance of national interests and state sovereignty and to insist that a "policy aimed at preserving sover-eignty and territorial integrity in a long-term perspective does not have any prospects" (Pastukhov 2000, 95-96; see also Saburov 2003; Sheinis 2003, 33; Shevtsova 2003; Yasin 2003).

It is suggested that Russia "gradually surrender its sovereignty to transna-tional corporations and international organizations, as do other civilized coun-tries" (Liberal'naya missiya 2001). Some authors propose the possibility of transferring the Kuril Islands to Japan in exchange for credits to be used for Siberian development and suggest transforming the Kaliningrad territory into a special zone of cooperation between Russia, Germany and Scandinavia (Rossiya i Zapad 2003). Along these lines was Sergeyev's (2001, 230) suggestion that it might be rational to transfer some attributes of state sovereignty to large and resources-rich regions when these regions are eager to acquire such attributes. According to Sergeyev's logic, the regions would then play the role of the "gates to the global world" (see also Zagladin 1998; Ionin 2001)

Other representatives of liberalism are more cautious. They agree that globalization weakens the foundation of the nation-state, but they put their emphasis on the contradictory and complicated nature of this process. Davydov, for instance, points to "the conflicting essence of globalization" and to "the need for transnational management of global processes," but he goes on to point that "the world is not yet ready for it, and it continues to attempt to manage these processes within the traditional framework of national and state institutions" (Davydov 2002, 28). He further suggests that nation-states continue to be behind all the key decisions regarding the nature of interaction in the international arena, even it takes place at the international institutional level. To illustrate his thinking, Davydov uses the example of the EU, which, in his views, is a an example of an emerging federation of states, rather than that of a super-state (2002, 10-11, 35).

Those Institutionalists that defend the values of nation-state and sovereignty in a changing world come closer to the positions of National Democrats. The latter continue to be convinced that, despite the growing process of globalization and international institutionalization, national communities continue to matter. Not only do such communities survive, but they find new forms of their cultural self-expression. Even in Europe, often used by liberal Institutionalists as the most obvious example of the erosion of sovereignty, nations and national sovereignty continue to play a principally important role. The position of Yuri Borko is quite illustrative in this respect. A prominent specialist in the area of European integration, Borko (1999) is convinced that such integration does not deny the role of nation-states. He makes a distinction between state functions and the forms their exercise takes. In his opinion, the facts of integration and eroding state responsibilities represent only one side of the process.

The other side has to do with transferring to the transnational level only some of those functions and responsibilities, specifically those that the state itself cannot effectively perform. The nation-state does not give up its sovereign rights; rather it is changing its approach to their realization. When confronted with the dilemma of defending some of its sovereign rights without having the full ability to exercise them or delegating those rights to the regional union level where they can be exercised more effectively, Western European states opted for the latter. While formally the state has lost parts of its sovereignty, it has also won by preserving some of its basic functions and relinquishing only some forms of their exercising (Borko 1999, 70).

Arguing against the thesis of the state erosion, Borko points to the growing number of states and the considerable expansion of their functions. He concludes by characterizing the thesis as nothing more than a myth and a deviation of scholarship from the real problem of state adaptation to changing conditions of its existence. Broadening of international cooperation is, in his view, one of the key conditions for success in such adaptation (1999, 67-68; also Salmin 2001).

Foreign policy orientations

Liberal schools also differ with regard to their analysis of Russia's foreign policy choices. Many believe that Russia should give up the illusions of a great power and accept its current status by agreeing to some limitations upon its independent foreign policy conduct (Liberal'naya missiya 2001). Modernizers, as well as some Institutionalists, insist that:

> if we do not promote the policy of strategic partnership with NATO, EU, as well as the West in general, and if we do not adopt the orientation toward Western and Euro-Atlantic values, Russia will be faced with inevitable marginalization (Ryzhov 2003).

Some disagreements do exist regarding the emphasis on a primarily American or primarily European orientation, but the majority is convinced that "a choice between Europe and America is not a real one, and the only choice is between a general Western orientation and the dead-end policy that had been in place before the 9/11" (Klyamkin 2003). This vision is reinforced by the argument of the country's cultural belongingness, whereby "Russia is a country of Judeo-Christian and European civilization, although it does represent a special branch within this civilization due to its special historical circumstances" (Sheinis 2003, 34).

As during the Kozyrev's period, Russia is recommended to gain distance from Asian states (Trenin 2001), especially China. It is argued that rapprochement with China is unfavorable and even dangerous for Russia. First, Russia can only play the role of a junior partner in such a rapprochement, given China's superior economic and demographic potential. Second, such an arrangement, especially if it is accompanied by cooperation with the so-called "rogue states," is likely to be viewed by the United States as aimed at confrontation with America and the West. As for independent foreign policy in the international arena, Russia cannot afford it due to its lack of resources (Saburov 2003; Yasin 2003; Sheinis 2003, 39-40). In other words, if Russia has to play the role of a junior partner, then the role of the "older" partner should be conceded to the most developed states of the West, or the Euro-Atlantic community in general (Ryzhov 2003; Shevtsova 2003; Fedorov 2001; Yasin 2003).

Moderate Institutionalists and National Democrats question the primacy of Western and European orientation in foreign policy. They take close to heart the fact that the largest mass of Russian territory stretches beyond the Ural Mountains and that a considerable part of Russians live in this non-European Russia. Based on this, the country is recommended not to turn away from its Eurasian identity but rather to seek cooperation with the nations of Asia and the Muslim world, not just Europe and America alone. National Democrats do not share the Modernizers' fear of China and perceive it as a country with no expansionist ambitions and one that is well integrated into international economic structures.[13] In addition, the supporters of a more diverse, or multi-vector foreign policy orientation point to the fact that the West is reluctant to cooperate with Russia, and therefore there are no sufficient grounds for pursuing a one-sided strategic relationships with the Western countries.[14]

---

[13] For a more detailed analysis of Russia's perceptions of China, see Lukin 2001.

The above formulated distinction between Modernizers and radical Institutionalists on the one hand, and National Democrats and moderate Institutionalists on the other, can be illustrated by comparing the views of Dmitri Trenin and Kamaludin Gadzhiev. The two are authors of recent books on Russian foreign policy and are influential representatives of different currents of Russian liberalism. Trenin's "The End of Eurasia" (2001) has been written to convince the reader that the age of Russia as the center of gravity in the region is over. The author views Eurasia as the area of traditional Russian power that can be historically traced to the tsardom of Muscovy, the empire, and the Soviet Union (Trenin 2001, 12). He maintains that because of pervasive external influences, especially those from the Western world and the West-initiated globalization, Russia now finds itself on the border between two worlds—the world of traditional geopolitical thinking and that of globalization—and must make a decisive choice. This choice, Trenin insists, must be in favor of cooperation with the West:

> Russia stands on the boundary between the post-modern and modern and even pre-modern world. It must make its choice. The only rational option is to fully stress Russia's European identity and engineer its gradual integration into a Greater Europe... a clear pro-Europe choice would facilitate the country's modernization, its adjustment to the 21st century world... Russia should first "build Europe" within its own borders. A failure to integrate would spell Russia's marginalization and possibly its disintegration. There is no longer an option of withdrawing into "Eurasia." (Trenin 2001, 319)

Trenin believes that Russia is a fundamentally European, not a Eurasian, country and therefore its "pro-European choice" should be quite natural. Russia must then become a role model of a European nation in the former Soviet world. Rather than trying to stabilize Eurasia or to integrate it into Russian bor-

---

[14] Liberals observe that "today's West does not have any willingness to cooperate, if by this we mean the existence of some well-defined strategy. Such a strategy is absent because its formulation is just as principally new for the West as it is for us" (Klyamkin 2003; Yasin 2003). In Salmin's (2001) formulation, "on September 11, Russia has chosen the West, but the West has not chosen Russia."

ders, as some other schools propose, Trenin sees Russia's strategy as one of "creative adjustment" to the newly emerged global and regional conditions. He argues that the West has already acquired a strong presence in Eurasia, whether Russians like it or not. While this may be a "harsh reality," Russia would do well in trying to make the best of it. The alternative, in Trenin's view, is to "become marginalized" without having a protective shell around its own borders (2001, 283).

Trenin proposes that Russia address problems of Eurasia through the direct involvement of the West, particularly the United States, which, as he concedes, increasingly replaces Russia as the "ultimate referee, protector, and donor" in the region (2001, 329). To him, language remains the only aspect of Russian presence in Eurasia (2001, 335); in all other respects, the country's retreat from the region is already a reality. Therefore, political realism requires that Russia undertakes nothing more than a series of carefully calibrated *ad hoc* responses to various ethnic, economic, political, and territorial conflicts in the region. To summarize Trenin's thinking, Russia has little choice but continue to retreat from the region in the face of the Western dominance. This position is close to views of such Western thinkers as Henry Kissinger, Francis Fukuyama and Zbigniew Brzezinski. While this is certainly a form of adjustment, it may be quite a stretch calling it a "creative" one.

Kamaludin Gadzhiyev's book *Introduction to Geopolitics* (2000) offers a different vision of Russia's geopolitical priorities. Gadzhiyev moves away from the old liberal philosophy of Russia's primary orientation to the West and takes seriously the strategic challenge of the country's presence in Eurasia. He believes in the necessity for Russia to develop a special Eurasian strategy, which requires moving beyond understanding the territorial space in terms of fixed boundaries and physical qualities and applying new notions of "economic, cultural-civilizational, informational, and other spaces" (Gadzhiyev 2000, 41-42). Unlike Trenin, Gadzhiyev views Russia as a key state of intermediate Eurasian location and does not link Russia's cultural identity exclusively to Europe or the West (2000, 321):

> While in the beginning of its reform, Russia's modernization
> meant its one-sided orientation on the "integration with

Europe," today's appreciation of revolutionary changes in information and telecommunication technologies, the world's polycentrism and the emergence of multiple centers— sources of the necessary knowledge, technology, and financial resources—opens to us much broader opportunities to learn from most advanced experiences and integrate into the world economy, without jeopardizing our national interest (Gadzhiyev 2000, 321).

Finally, Gadzhiyev argues for extending the notion of Eurasia beyond geo-economics and into independent political and cultural area, as well. According to him, Russia's role is in building a transportation or trade "bridge" between Europe and Asia, in bridging and pacifying European and Asian civilizations, as well as maintaining a delicate equilibrium among a wide variety of ethnic groups. After the end of the Soviet era and Russia's period of relative external isolation, it must formulate its foreign policy goals and interests anew to help stabilizing the region, while at the same staying open to variety of economic and cultural influences (Gadzhiyev 2000, 316-23). The fact that Eurasia is so culturally diverse and currently unstable politically does not mean that it is doomed to be a battlefield for conflict between different ethnicities and civilizations, as Huntington's (1996) "clash of civilizations" scenario implies (Gadzhiyev 2000, 400).[15] Instead, it may become an arena for practicing a mutually fertile dialogue and cooperative economic and security arrangements. Gadzhiyev's vision of Eurasia is then that of an open region that should at the same time serve as an independent political, economic, and cultural entity. In addition to the West, Gadzhiyev proposes that Russia cooperates with China, Japan, both Koreas, and other states of the region in building an appropriate collective security system in Eurasia and outside.

4. The Future of Russian Liberal IR

Russian Liberalism has emerged as an interesting and important current of international theory that has been consistently critical of Realist and Isolation-

---

[15] Fore a more detailed analysis of Russian perception of the Huntington thesis, see Tsygankov 2004.

ist schools in intellectual and political discourse. Publications by liberals have greatly enhanced the growth of social science literature. Liberals have pointed out various deficiencies of Realist approaches, such as excessive attention to the role of power capabilities and traditional geopolitical factors in foreign policy. They have been correct in emphasizing some new phenomena of world politics, such as growing significance of non-state actors and changes concerning the institution of the national state. Finally, they have been right to argue the urgency of a more successful management of globalization's processes, to promote more effective mechanisms of addressing common threats through international cooperation, and to advocate Russia's increasing integration into the world.

At the same time, the discussions among liberals after the Soviet disintegration have revealed some principal disagreements, which cannot be easily resolved. These disagreements are especially acute between Modernizers and National Democrats, but the general fault-line of discussions often divides Modernizers and radical Institutionalists, on the one hand, and moderate Institutionalists and National Democrats, on the other. Immediately after the Soviet collapse, the first group had dominated in the intellectual and political discourse of Russia, while the second group had resorted to the status of opposition. The Liberal discussions are now going through their second round, and at this time against the backdrop of considerable weakening of both Modernizers and radical Institutionalists, and of a strengthening of Realists, and of some modest increase in the activity of National Democrats and moderate Institutionalists. The defeat of the first group has revealed all too well the depth of disagreements within the Liberal camp.

	Modernizers and radical Institutionalists	Moderate Institutionalists and National Democrats
World order	West-centric	Pluralist
Sovereignty and national interest	Looses its significance	Significant, but must be reformulated
Foreign policy orientation	Pro-Western	Multi-vector

The table summarizes these contradictions and demonstrates all the difficulties of overcoming these disagreements. Such difficulties are related, above all, to the intellectual dogmatism of Westernizers, who often deny the importance of some principal phenomena of the contemporary world, such as the state, power multipolarity, and cultural diversity. Instead of trying to rethink or reformulate these phenomena and their work under contemporary conditions, Westernizers often deny them altogether under the pretext of the new era of Western "globalization."

It is, therefore, hard to arrive to anything more definitive than to the conclusion about an uncertain future of Russian Liberalism. The disagreements analyzed in the essay are too serious and are not likely to be softened, unless the West itself undergoes some considerable transformation. Until the belief in the superiority of West-centered development and—with it—the rejection of alternative paths in historical development prevails in attitudes and behavior of the West and the United States, the above-identified contradictions will continue to be central in the Russian Liberal discourse. Resolving these contradictions will hardly be possible. Such is the drama although hardly the tragedy of contemporary Russian Liberalism.

As for the future of Russian Liberalism, we associate it primarily with representatives of the second group. Both moderate Institutionalists and National Democrats work on reevaluating the variety of world development paths in earnest and without denying their potential using the rhetoric of the "end of history" or the triumph of Western market democracies. Their main objective should be consistency in moving in this new direction without slipping over to the Realist vision. A continuous critique of Westernization is of no less importance, especially when the latter demonstrates intolerance in politics and dogmatism in theory. Undoubtedly, this will require mobilization of considerable intellectual efforts.

These efforts are only in their beginning, but in the future, they could receive a considerable social support. Until the West attempts to stay engaged—even as passively as today—rather than relying on its "bombs' arguments," the social support for the Realist and Isolationist thinking and Russian politics will not be robust. In the meantime, the Russian middle class is gradually getting stronger, and this group does not favor either militarism or confrontation with the outside world. This group also supports economic and political reforms consistent with the values of national identity and independent statehood. The middle class of Russia's traditionally left society is a now fairly broad group and includes not only small and medium size businesses. It also includes those strata of state bureaucracy and workers of state enterprises that are ready to support considerable state involvement in national democratic development.

References

Abolin, O. A. 1995. Otkaz ot printsipa "absolyutnogo suvereniteta." Polis 1.

Adamishin, A. L. 2002. Na puti k mirovomu pravitel'stvu. Rossiya v global'noi politike 1.

Borko, Yu. A. 1999. Problema natsional'nogo suvereniteta. Kosmopolis.

Brzezinski, Z. 1998. The Grand Chessboard. Basic Books, New York.

Bull, H. and A. Watson, eds. 1984. The Expansion of International Society. Clarendon Press, Oxford.

Bunin, I. 2003. Vystupleniye. In: Rossiya i Zapad. Discussion organized by the foundation "Liberal'naya missiya" and Moscow Carnegie Center. June 28. http://www.liberal.ru/sitan.asp?Num=115 <accessed on August 20, 2003>.

Buzgalin, A. 2002. Russia and America: A New Twist in the Confrontation? Prism 8, 3 http://www.jamestown.com <accessed on April 2, 2002>.

Cox, R. W. 1995. Civilizations: Encounters and Transformations. Studies in Political Economy 47 (3).

Davydov Yu. P. 2002. Norma protiv sily. Problema mirouregulirovaniya. Institut SShA i Kanady, Moskva.

Federov, Yu. 2001. Vystupleniye. In: Rossiya v poiskakh strategicheskoi pozitsii. Discussion organized by the foundation "Liberal'naya missiya," www. liberal.ru.sitan.asp?Num33 <accessed on January 14, 2002>.

Fedorov, V. 2002. Vperyed, k ideologii? Nezavisimaya gazeta, 18 February.

Furman, D. 1992. Rossiyskiye demokraty i raspad soyuza. Vek XX i mir 1.

Gadziyev, K. S. 2000. Vvedeniye v geopolitiku. Logos, Moskva.

Gaidar, Ye. 1997. Gosudarstvo i evolyutsiya. Yevraziya, Moskva.

Gefter, M. Ya. 1991. Iz tekh i etikh let. Progress, Moskva.

Gorbachev, M., ed. 2003. Grani globalizatsii. Al'pina, Moskva.

Huntington, S. 1996. The Clash of Civilizations and the Remaking of World Order. Simon & Shuster, NY.

Ionin, L. 2001. Vystupleniye. In: Rossiya v poiskakh strategicheskoi pozitsii. Discussion organized by the foundation "Liberal'naya missiya," www. liberal.ru.sitan.asp?Num33 <accessed on January 14, 2002>.

Kapustin, B. 1996. "Natsional'nyi interes" kak konservativnaya utopiya. Svobodnaya mysl' 3.

Kapustin, B. 1998. Sovremennost' kak predmet politcheskoi teorii. ROSSPEN, Moskva.

Kara-Murza, A. 2001. Na perekrestke politiki i nauki. Polis 6, http:// www.politstudies.ru/universum/esse/8kmz.htm#17 <accessed on February 14, 2002>.

Kiselev, V., Klyamkin, I. (eds.) 1989. Sotsializm mezhdu proshlym i budushchim. Progress, Moskva.

Klyamkin, I. 2001. Vystupleniye. In: Rossiya v poiskakh strategicheskoi pozitsiyi. Discussion organized by the foundation "Liberal'naya missiya," www. liberal.ru.sitan.asp?Num33 <accessed on January 14, 2002>.

Kortunov, S. 1998. Imperskoye i natsionalnoye v rossiyskom soznanii. Mezhdunarodnaya zhizn' 5, 6.

Kortunov, S. 2002. Stanovleniye novogo mirovogo poryadka. Mezhdunarodnaya zhizn' 6.

Kozyrev, A. 1992. Preobrazhennaya Rossiya v novom mire. Mezhdunarodnaya zhizn' 3-4.

Kozyrev, A. 1995. Preobrazheniye. Mezhdunarodnyye otnosheniya, Moskva.

Krasin, Yu. A., (ed.) 1996. Natsional'nyye interesy. Gorbachev-fond, Moskva.

Kulagin, V. M. 2000. Mir v XX veke: mnogopolyusnyi balans sil ili global'nyi Pax Democratica. Polis 1.

Lebedeva, M. 2003. Mirovaya politika. Aspekt-Press, Moskva.

Liberal'naya missiya Foundation. 2001. Rossiya v poiskakh strategicheskoi pozitsiyi. Discussion organized by the foundation "Liberal'naya missiya," www. liberal.ru.sitan.asp?Num33 <accessed on January 14, 2002>.

Light, M. 1996. Foreign Policy Thinking. In: Internal Factors in Russian Foreign Policy, edited by Neil Malcolm et al. Oxford University Press, Oxford.

Linklater, A. 1998. The Transformation of Political Community. Polity Press, Oxford.

Lukin, V. 2001. Vystupleniye. In: Rossiya v poiskakh strategicheskoi pozitsiyi. Discussion organized by the foundation "Liberal'naya missiya," www. liberal.ru.sitan.asp?Num33 <accessed on January 14, 2002>.

Makarenko, B. 2000. Kto soyuzniki Rossii? No publisher information, Moskva.

Milyukov, P. 1992 [1896]]. Ocherki po istorii russkoi kul'tury. Progress, Moskva.

Panarin, A. 1995. Yevraziyski proyekt v mirosistemnom kontekste. Vostok 3.

Panarin, A. 1998. Revansh istorii. Logos, Moskva.

Panarin, A. 2000. Global'noye politicheskoye prognozirovaniye. Algoritm, Moskva.

Pantin, V. I. 2002. Rossiya v neustoichivom mire. In: Mesto i rol' Rossii v transfomiruyuscheysya sisteme mezhdunarodnykh otnosheniyi. No publisher information, Nizhniyi Novgorod.

Pastukhov, V. B. 2000. Natsional'nyi i gosudarstvennyi interesy Rossii. Polis 1.

Polyakov, L. V. 2000. Epokha burzhuaznogo pragmatizma. Polis 1.

Putin, V. 2001. Speech to the German parliament (in Russian), 25 September, at: www.kremlin.ru.

Rossiya i Zapad. 2003. Discussion organized by the foundation "Liberal'naya missiya" and Moscow Carnegie Center. June 28. http://www.liberal.ru/ sitan.asp?Num=115 <accessed on August 20, 2003>.

Ryzhov, Yu. 2003. Vystupleniye. In: Rossiya i Zapad. Discussion organized by the foundation "Liberal'naya missiya" and Moscow Carnegie Center. June 28. http://www.liberal.ru/sitan.asp?Num=115 <accessed on August 20, 2003>.

Saburov, Ye. 2003. Vystupleniye. In: Rossiya i Zapad. Discussion organized by the foundation "Liberal'naya missiya" and Moscow Carnegie Center. June 28. http://www.liberal.ru/sitan.asp?Num=115 <accessed on August 20, 2003>.

Salmin, A. M. 1994. Dezintegratsiya bipolyarnogo mira i perspektivy novogo mirovogo poryadka. Polis 4.

Salmin, A. M. 2001. Rossiya v novom yevropeyskom poryadke. In: Mir i Rossiya na poroge XXI veka. No publisher information, Moskva.

Sergeyev, V. M. 1999. Gosudarstvennyi suverenitet i evolyutsiya sistemy mezhdunarodnykh otnosheniyi. Kosmopolis 1.

Sergeyev, V. M. 2001. Ekonomicheskiye tsentry sily na poroge XXI veka. In: Mir i Rossiya na poroge XXI veka. No publisher information, Moskva.

Sergunin, A. A. 2000. Russian post-Communist Foreign Policy Thinking at the Cross-roads. Journal of International Relations and Development 3 (3).

Shakhnazarov, G. 1998. Miroporyadok tsivilizatsi? Pro et Contra 3 (4).

Sheinis, V. L. 2003. Natsional'nyye interesy i vneshnyaya politika Rossii. MEMO 4.

Shevtsova, L. 2003. Vystupleniye. In: Rossiya i Zapad. Discussion organized by the foundation "Liberal'naya missiya" and Moscow Carnegie Center. 28 June. http://www.liberal.ru/sitan.asp?Num=115 <accessed on August 20, 2003>.

Shlapentokh, V. 1998. "Old," "New" and "Post" Liberal Attitudes Towards the West: From Love to Hate. Communist and Post-Communist Studies 31 (3).

Trenin, D. 2001. The End of Eurasia. Carnegie Center, Moscow.

Tsygankov, A. P. 1997. From Liberal Internationalism to Revolutionary Expansionism. Mershon International Studies Review 41 (2).

Tsygankov, A. P. 2001. The Final Triumph of the Pax Americana? Communist and Post-Communist Studies 33 (3).

Tsygankov, A. P. 2003. Mastering Space in Eurasia. Communist and Post-Communist Studies 35 (1).

Tsygankov, A. P. 2004. Whose World Order? University Press of Notre Dame, Notre Dame.

Yasin, Ye. 2003. Vystupleniye. In: Rossiya i Zapad. Discussion organized by the foundation "Liberal'naya missiya" and Moscow Carnegie Center. 28 June. http://www.liberal.ru/sitan.asp?Num=115 <accessed on August 20, 2003>.

Yavlinski, G. 2002. Dver' v Yevropu nakhoditsya v Vashingtone. Obshchaya gazeta, 16 May, www.og.ru <accessed on June 12, 2003>.

Zagladin, N. V. 2000. Novyi mirovoi besporyadok i vneshnyaya politika Rossii. MEMO 1.

V. Studies of globalization and equity in post-Soviet Russia

Mikhail V. Il'yin

1. The interface of globalization and equity: The relevance of cleavages

The interface between globalization and equity is both perplexing and conspic-uous. Its promise and fragility are not to be overlooked. In fact, equity in this age cannot be analyzed without full use of global interactions and encourage-ment. Similarly globalization would not realize its human potential unless it promotes equity. It is not by chance that the UNDP Report for 1999 highlights equity as a crucial qualification of globalization—"less disparity within and between nations, not more"—along five other—ethics, inclusion, human secu-rity, sustainability, and development.

In the global context, desire to ensure a positive interface of globalization and equity can hardly be challenged. But in more specific contexts and in indi-vidual situations this general principle may find various and often conflicting interpretations. While agreeing on the general principles, people act differently because of political, social, economic, cultural, and even linguistic cleavages. It was Norwegian political scientist Stein Rokkan (1921-1979) who designed research instruments of cleavage analysis. Rokkan constructed numerous variations in cleavages schemes, but from an early date these schemes were similar in that they distinguished sharply between economic cleavages on the one hand and cultural cleavages on the other. They also sought to differentiate within each of these categories according to the dimension of center-periphery conflict.[1]

In the progression of his work, Rokkan established that major cleavages emerged as the historical result of interaction between at least four revolu-tions: the reformation, the national revolution, the industrial revolution, and the international (i.e. Russian) revolution. They are respectively *church—state*, *center—periphery*, *land—industry*,[2] *owners—workers* cleavages. According to the famous "freezing proposition,"[3] whenever a cleavage emerged, it affected politics of later ages.

For practical reasons, Rokkanian research had been limited to Europe.[4] To better understand the differences in interpretation of the globalization-equity interface, we have to extend cleavage analysis beyond Europe. From this perspective, one cannot overlook the clash of imperialist and anti-imperialist policies that resulted in the de-colonization revolution and the *metropolis—colony* cleavage. One should also not miss the collision of mass control and human rights aspirations resulting in the 1989 de-totalitarianization revolution with its *network—hierarchy* cleavage. Finally, one might also note a discrepancy between industrial and postindustrial ways of life and the emerging information (or rather creativity) revolution with its *capital—knowledge* cleavage.

The last but not least important global cleavage dimension is linguocultural, or as some might say "civilizational." These linguocultural cleavages make the interface of globalization and equity particularly problematic and offer a perspective that is quite different from those of English-speaking nations. Russians and Russian-speaking post-Soviet citizens are a case in point.

What cleavages are relevant to the Russian interpretation of globalization and equity?

Probably the most important one is neither among the Rokkanian cleavages nor among the three additional ones that had been prompted by develop-

---

[1] Initially Rokkan noted the gap between the formal extension of voting rights and their actual use, then the specific cleavages that emerged with new mass organizations, and the role of the mass media, whether in reinforcing or cross-cutting political allegiances (Rokkan 1959; Rokkan & Torsvik 1960). Further he studied sharp divisions related to the abandonment of absolute monarchy, the extension of the suffrage, and effects of introduction of various electoral systems as well as to religion, class etc. (Rokkan 1966; 1967; 1968).

[2] Or the *Agraria—Industria* in terms of Fred W. Riggs (1957).

[3] Older cleavages might persist even when new issues might temporarily hide them. Thus, "the [European] party systems of the 1960s reflect, with few but significant exceptions, the cleavage structures of the 1920s" (Rokkan & Lipset 1967, 50).

[4] The first two revolutions and sets of cleavages are exclusively West European. The third is initially and, as a result, mainly West European. Only the forth one can be considered an international one, but it is also West European in its origin and "bourgeois" logic.

ments of the last century. But it is crucial to many, if not most, countries of the world. It is essentially the primordial *authority—people* cleavage. Its centrality to the Russian world view and politics is obvious. Yet until recently it has never been properly analyzed. Only in the 1990s did Fursov and Pivovarov undertake a very daring attempt to unveil the mystique of *Russkaya vlast'* (Russian Power)[5] in a series of publications (see especially Pivovarov and Fursov 2001). The cleavage does not abruptly separate persons belonging to *vlast'* (authority) from the rest or *Naseleniye* (Population) in Fursov-Pivovarov's terms. Both *vlast'* and *naseleniye* or *narod* feel deeply entwined in love-hate relations that are highly irrational and ambiguous. With all its problems, the *authority—people* cleavage is extremely operational and effective in the Russian context. Being a core cleavage, it dominates and even shapes the four Rokkanian cleavages that had emerged as the result of "modernization" efforts of *vlast'* or more specifically of *pravitel'stvo* (government), which is "the only European in Russia," according to the poet Alexandr Pushkin.

Internationally, the *owners—workers* or rather the *bourgeoisie—proletariat* cleavage had become indispensable during Soviet times. It served as the ideological facade for the revolutionary or intelligentsia vision of the *authority—people* cleavage. While the hegemony of world capitalism had been recognized as the actual *vlast'* at the global level, the USSR and world socialism were seen as both its opponent (leader of global "people") and the would-be global *vlast'*. This cleavage easily intermingled with the international *metropolis—colony* cleavage in the anti-imperialist liberation world view. Other international cleavages, such as the *network—hierarchy* and the *capital—knowledge*, only partially apply to Russia, since it is only a partial participant of modernization and globalization processes.

---

[5]   In Russian, the word власть (vlast') means both "power" and "authority." According to Pivovarov and Fursov (2001), in the Russian system, *samoderzhavie* or autocracy embodies total concentration of *vlast'*, depriving all possible actors of their *sub'ektnost'* or ability for independent action.

2. Globalization and equity in the Russian perspective

Russian political scientists have recently begun to explore anew their country's cultural characteristics. There are hardly any studies of what the notions of globalization, equity, justice, fairness, or honesty mean in the Russian context. One might suggest, however, that Russian visions of globalization and equity are culture- and language-specific. In Russian the word "*globalizatsiya* "(globalization) sounds like a technical term. To most Russians, the term is socially abstract and devoid of any practical everyday meaning. So are most other words of the –*ations* family, e.g. "*democratization,*" "*legitimatization,*" and others. Not yet taken in, the notion of globalization is often seen by Russians as some kind of *deus ex machina*. To West-friendly Russians, it appears as the ultimate device that could bring about solutions to all possible problems—very much what the notion of "*revolution"* was to the first Soviet generations. Those Russians that are hostile to the West see it as a *daemon ex machina* or at least as a *malum ex machina*. In between, there is a growing sector of the public that considers *globalization* an objective process, resembling *amelioration* or *deterioration* as the case may be.

The word "*equity"* is different. To begin with, not too many English-speaking Russians know the word. Many who do speak English find it exotic and difficult to translate into Russian.[6] Few people understand its connotations or know the legal meaning of the English term. But that does not mean that Russians, even those not versed in English, have no idea of equity. To many Russians and Russian-speaking post-Soviet citizens, equity is a very broad notion, even broader than the concept of "*justice.*" One can say it is a kind of equivalent to the English "*fairness"*[7] but it is not identical to it. In my view, the best Russian equivalent for "*equity"* would be "*честность"* (honesty).[8] It is a special kind of

---

6   A standard English-Russian dictionary would give Russian equivalents of "*spravedli-vost'"* (justice) "*nepredvzyatost'"* (impartiality). As legal term it is translated as "*pravo spravedlivosti"* (law of justice).
7   The first English synonym for "*equity"* is "*fairness.*"
8   Although the word "*spravedlivost'"* (justice) is typically used in the globalization and equity debate, it actually expresses a different notion of "*chestnost'"* (honesty).

entitlement that is based on its integral worth, with a special emphasis on its contribution to or sacrifice for a more general good.

The majority of Russians feel that Russia is entitled to respect and recognition for its accomplishments by the rest of the world. The reasons are diverse and numerous, depending on individuals' various and often opposite ideological allegiances. Some would rest their claim on the country's sacrifice in the Second World War. Others would point to the Gorbachev-initiated voluntary renunciation of the superpower status for the sake of "universal human values." Others still might claim that Russia always provided more to others then it got in return. You could hardly find a Russian who would disagree that his or her country is treated unfairly for all the good it has done.

Whatever linguistic, cultural, religious or any other limitations may influence our visions of reality or behavior, all nations and individuals are able to grasp universally relevant ideas and practices.[9] This is true of differentiating between economic and cultural values or between electoral and political power by the English-speaking persons. This is equally true for the Russian understanding of globalization, equity, and their interface. However, we should not ignore the possible impact of language, culture, and religion on political conceptualization and behavior. Still, with all their cultural specificity, Russians are very much aware of globalization and equity problems. Globalization has made a profound impact on Russia. Its effects have been exacerbated by the collapse of the USSR and destabilization of the successor states. These effects have been mainly negative. Yet quite a number of Russian institutions and individuals, particularly in Moscow and other major cities, have managed to adapt to globalization and make good use of it. Generally speaking, Russia, probably more than any other successor state, demonstrates the clash of conflicting

---

[9] Some time ago I used as a point of departure a passing remark by Ronald Reagan to BBC Channel 4 (October 29th, 1985) that Russians have no word or idea of freedom and made a comparative study of various national ways of conceptualizing freedom. My main conclusion was that freedom is a universal property of human existence, and that it is conceptualized in various ways by all languages, cultures and polities within the scope of the study. The study remains unpublished. Some parts of it appeared as a chapter in a book on key political concepts (Il'yin 1997a, 41-79).

tendencies. In the Russian case, effects of globalization on equity may be more diverse and mixed then in other successor countries.

The problem of the globalization-equity conflict seems most topical to any concerned Russian citizen. The older generations are inclined to perceive social developments in the light of the earlier identified cleavages--*authority vs. people* or *bourgeoisie vs. proletariat* or *metropolis vs. colony*--with all accompanying interpretations. Still the relevance of more recent and essentially global cleavages--the *network—hierarchy* and the *capital—knowledge*-- as well as the spread of the very idea of globalization, is gradually, and sometimes rather rapidly, winning over the younger generations by actively incorporating them into transnational socially-productive activities.

3. The beginning of the globalization and equity debate in post-Soviet Russia

The debate on globalization and equity has been growing in Russia since the late 1990s. It has three main dimensions. The broadest dimension rests within the regular media. The media treatment of the interface between globalization and equity is very superfluous and hectic. In most cases, media treatments are ideologically motivated and can be traced to the major cleavages described in sections 1 and 2 of this paper. In contrast, the most relevant dispute is confined to narrow audiences and runs in rather limited scholarly circles. Its relations to major cleavages is less evident.

An example of crude bias is displayed by a celebrated professor of economics and formerly the mayor of Moscow Gavriyil Popov (2000), who has published a short article in the Russian tabloid *Moskovskiyi komsomolets*. The article presents globalization as "catchword of the present American administration for framing planetary order in the XXI century." According to Popov, the appropriate response to the collapse of the bipolar world order would have been "the second edition of the Marshall plan for Russia." Instead, Washington defended a plan of its own named "globalization." The plan leads to a pyramid-like world order with USA at its top. Next to it are six major countries that form a kind of a council for the world's leader. The second layer is formed by prosperous countries of secondary rank—Sweden, Spain, Austria, Israel etc. And, at last, at the base of the pyramid are the Third World countries (Popov 2000). Black and white statements are typical of the debate on globalization and equity in post-communist Russia. Often globalization and equity are interpreted as absolutely incompatible, and globalization is viewed as a result of a conspiracy. Such a story would not deserve any serious consideration if it were not striving to dominate the discourse on globalization and equity. It is both widespread and ardently promoted by the people claiming to define Russian political thinking. An emblematic figure for this is Alexandr Panarin. This author of numerous publications (1998, 1999a, 2000a, 2002) that unveil immoral conspiracies of the Western liberals and their Russian henchmen is a professor of politics at Moscow State University and the bearer of numerous titles, degrees, and honors. To him, globalization is associated with "social asymmetry" (Panarin 2002, 61) or "new and global segregation of peoples into the chosen and the wretched, into the omnipotent center and the oppressed periphery" (Panarin 2002, 12) by "the dictatorship of globalism" (Panarin 2002, 63). One can easily distinguish the communist or anti-globalist cleavage formula in the cited text.

Alexandr Panarin is highly critical of globalization because of its totalitarian sway. He condemns what he views as the "American totalitarian complex" (Panarin 2002, 111-119) and "economic totalitarianism" (Panarin 2002, 119-125). Instead, he insists the world should uphold the system of nation-states and embrace a plurality of alternatives as the main hopes for the future. One of his preferred scenarios is the "restoration of a civic consensus on the basis of exclusion of the nomadic diaspora" (Panarin 2002, 362-396). The second one is "the alternative globalism" (Panarin 2002, 396-408), which is rather bleak and gloomy:

> A harsh and dramatic epoch lies ahead of us.... the anthropological revolution of Americanism, designed to implant a singe "liberal type" to dominate the planet must be condemned as a failed adventure. ... A different type of personality is needed, one awakened to planetary responsibility. A great spiritual and political authority (vlast') is needed to promote this type. It is the school of new ascetic upbringing. In

all probability, it will be a clear global alternative to the present "liberal" Americanocentrism. It implies a new shift of the global political center from Atlantics to Eurasia. (Panarin 2002, 407-408).

Panarin avoids citing his opponents, and one can hardly avoid the impression that they are invented persons and convenient whipping-boys for his eloquent criticism. Usually he speaks of anonymous globalists with rare qualifications like "American," "Western," "Americanocentered," "Jewish" and "liberal." In his recent book (2002) Panarin makes only one direct reference to his opponent, a well-known sociologist Leonid Ionin. This liberal scholar has been selected to embody all the vice of "liberal Westernizing intelligentsia," but he is a kind of mirror image of Panarin himself. In fact, Ionin's claims sound as harsh and essentialist as Panarin's own. The only difference is that he inverts the arguments and defends the opposite side of the same cleavage. Social scientists who enter the public debate on globalization are inclined to gross simplifications. They often fall victim to fitting rather bluntly and primitively to the cleavage structures of public opinion. Their analysis will become subtle and balanced only when they demonstrate openness to the varieties of existing divisions and lines of cross-cleavage.

4. New centers of globalization studies in Russian political science

Marxist universalistic thinking, with all its negative effects, facilitated the emergence of "global thinking." Often Marxism has been associated with humanistic concerns and genuinely global vision of political developments. Since the early 1970s, political scientists and international relations scholars developed a strong interest in studying such global issues, as the environment, population growth, arms race, and others. In the 1980s, debates on post-industrial and information societies became very topical. The last but not least significant in its impact was the late 1980s' debate on Gorbachev's "new political thinking." Unfortunately this promising idea was soon plagued by ideological verbiage and was not developed in any substantive terms.[10] As a result, Russian

---

[10] It was around 1989 that I personally had to give up my plans for writing a book on the new political thinking as a frame for a new epistemological synthesis.

scholars began to discuss globalization issues later than the West despite their long-standing tradition of "thinking globally." Well in the mid-1990s Russian scholars were not yet directly engaged with globalization, but instead continued to discuss modernization and modernization-related issues. Only in 1997-1998 did the word "globalization" began to appear in the titles of media and scholarly publications. The year 1999 became a watershed that marked a massive expansion of globalization debate. It was only natural that, at its initial stage, the main efforts were directed at attempting to understand the meaning of Western globalization-related ideas. Most of the articles published at that time interpret and reinterpret ideas of foreign political scientists (Bogaturov 1999, 47).

A very important role in this work belonged to the *Institute of Scientific Information on Social Sciences (INION)* of the Russian Academy of Sciences. Since the mid-1990s, INION had been introducing Russian social scientists to reviews, and summaries of major foreign studies of globalization. This is of particular importance since most of Russian political scientists are not versed in foreign languages.[11] In 2002, INION, in collaboration with the Gorbachev Foundation (see below), released its most significant collection of reviews and summaries of globalization papers. The publication consists of three volumes. The first is devoted to the concept of globalization, with its complexity and numerous dimensions, as well as the change in international relations and the role of the state. The second one covers mainly economic aspects, but includes sections on the welfare state and policymaking (corporate policies, interface of local, regional and global policies, and others). The third volume is concerned with other aspects of globalization—cultural, ethnic, demographic, ecological, educational, and so on.

Another important "translator" of globalization ideas is the *Center for Post-Industrial Studies* created by Vladislav Inozemtsev. Although Inozemtsev is critical of the concept of globalization and believes that the term "post-industri-

---

[11] According to estimates of the late 90s' only 2-5% of Russian political scientists actually read papers of their foreign colleagues in the original. Although the situation is slowly improving, the majority of Russian political scientists badly rely on translations, summaries and reviews of literature in other languages.

alism" better describes the present day developments, his work (Inozemstev 1995, 1998a, 1998b) has been instrumental in promoting globalization studies in Russia. One should also not overlook a body of articles reviewing research of foreign scholars on globalization (Kollontai 2002; Veber 2001). They have played an important role in familiarizing Russian scholars with the main ideas of the globalization debate.

Independent research on political globalization began as early as the mid-1990s at the department of Political Science of *Moscow State Institute of International Relations (MGIMO)*. Initially, the core MGIMO team had been formed by Andrei Mel'vil', Ivan Tyulin, Viktor Sergeyev, Alexei Shestopal, Alexei Bogaturov, Alexei Voskresenski, Marina Lebedeva, Andrei Volodin, and myself. We had launched a series of discussions that became instrumental in drawing the attention of Russian political scientists to globalization. Unfortunately, many of the debates of 1995-1997 were not recorded and remain unpublished. But already in 1996, the MGIMO team organized a joint US-Russian seminar in Moscow on global political and social changes. The seminar's materials have subsequently been published as a separate volume (Mel'vil' 1997), which focused on political aspects of the globalization phenomenon and covered a wide range of issues from philosophy and culture to demography and health.

Another important center for globalization studies emerged at the *Gorbachev Foundation*. In 1997, the Foundation launched a series of projects on the subject, with Mikhail Gorbachev deeply involved in their planning and running. Well over two hundred leading experts, as well as numerous politicians and public figures from various countries, participated in conferences and round-table discussions in Moscow, Boston, Frankfurt-on-Main, Amman, Calgary, Almaty, Karlsruhe, and so on. In the process, two teams of Russian experts developed and published a series of research papers, resulting in a book (Gorbachev 2002) that addressed economic, political, and cultural dimensions of globalization and Russia's role in it.

The third important center was established at the *Institute of World Economy and International Relations (IMEMO)* of the Russian Academy of Sciences. As I understand it, the institute began to study globalization as early as the mid-1990s. Between 1997 and 1999, IMEMO organized a series of seminars on postindustrial studies an effort which allowed it to emerge as a major center of globalization expertise for a much wider political science community. A series of discussions resulted in a conference held in autumn 1999 and a published four-volume collection (Postindustrial'nyi mir 1999; see also Postindustrial'nyi mir i Rossiya 2000). Theoretically, the work of IMEMO has been most influenced by the world-system paradigm. It is only natural that the *metropolis—colony* and *center—periphery* cleavages shaped the direction and the nature of the argument presented by most of the collection's authors, particularly in the first two volumes. The first volume of the collection was titled "General issues of the post-industrial epoch," but the authors often preferred to describe "post-industrial developments" as "globalization." The word itself appeared in the title of the next volume—"Globalization and the periphery." The third volume was devoted to the "special case of Russia," while the fourth—"World culture on the threshold of the 21st century"—addressed cultural dimensions of globalization and relied heavily on post-modernist vocabulary.

Since 2000, globalization has also emerged as a very important topic for Russian journals of Political and Social Sciences, most prominently *Cosmopolis 99*, *Pro et Contra*, and *MEMO* (World Economy and International Relations).

5. Main approaches to the study of globalization in
Russian political science

The situation in Russian Social Sciences is one that is not conducive to objective studies of globalization. Vladislav Inozemtsev confesses in his book that Russian social scientists "relate to the West with a combination of respect … and hostility," which causes "an unprecedented moral unease" about globalization studies (Inozemstev 1999, xiii). Nevertheless, some Russian scholars have developed sober and serious approaches to globalization. One could agree with Bogaturov (1999, 47) who believes that Russian scholars are not overly negative in their estimates of globalization in general, but they do tend to be critical of some of its Western proponents who exaggerate its positive consequences (Volodin and Shirokov 1999; Kollontai 1999). Still, the problem is not whether the attitude towards globalization is positive, or negative, or mixed. The questions essential in the Russian context are different. What is globalization? Is it relevant to development of Russia? How can one study it? The answers may depend to a great extent on the cleavage structure described in sections 1–3. Although serious scholars remain relatively unaffected by the pressures of public opinion, they do continue to value cleavages as an analytical tool.

The fundamental or primordial *authority—people* cleavage is particularly appealing to the faction of scholars who may be called post-modernists. This group rebels against authority, a tradition typical of the Russian intelligentsia, and promotes emancipation and resistance to the centers of global domination. Such an approach has not produce any problem-solving knowledge but it has proven effective as a political and moral philosophical critique of globalization. Some work of the INION team, like *Postindustrial'nyi mir*, and the writings of Boris Kapustin (2001a, 2001b) may be considered as the best examples of post-modern ethical critique of globalization.

The *church—state* cleavage appeals to students of political cultures and proponents of civilization studies. The works of Boris Yerasov (2001) and S. Panarin (2002)[12] can be cited as examples of this scholarly direction.

The *center—periphery* cleavage and, to a lesser extent, the *land—industry* cleavage have been topical to economic development students since the Soviet times. Naturally, many scholars had been greatly influenced by the neo-Marxist world-system methodology. This approach is wide-spread, and the IMEMO team has made particularly good use of it. Still, in the Russian context the world-system analysis is more a mode of historical interpretation rather than a guide to innovative research or a source of advancement for practical knowledge. For practical reasons, many of the method's champions had turned to Kondrat'ev's cycles and neo-institutionalism for research insights, an approach that proved rather fruitful (see Lapkin and Pantin 1999; Pantin 1997; Pantin 2002).

The *owners—workers* or rather the *bourgeoisie—proletariat* cleavage appeals to the more traditional brand of Marxists. It has many zealots in university departments, particularly outside of Moscow, but it has not produced

---

[12] Not to be confused with Alexandr Panarin mentioned in section 3.

much in the way of research results. Nevertheless, some scholars of neo-Marxist orientation have done interesting work in trying to develop an alternative vision of globalization or "*alterglobalism*" (Buzgalin 2001) and made valuable contributions to the study of mass protests against globalization (Kagarlitski 2002).

Orientalists, or scholars studying the East, have strongly been influenced by the *metropolis—colony* cleavage. In addition to the already mentioned writings of Volodin and Shirokov, one should mention the rather exotic reinterpretation of global developments by the Africanist Alexandr Neklessa (2000), who has developed a conceptual map of the globe that emphasizes the "New North," with its moving "islands," the "Deep South," and the remaining "pieces" of the former East, West, North, and South.

The *network—hierarchy* cleavage inspires those researchers who are interested in the 1989 anti-totalitarian revolution and the democratic tendencies in global politics. One can find such scholars all over the scene, but the faction most consistently following this approach is the MGIMO team.

The information (creativity) revolution, with its *capital—knowledge* cleavage, has its own proponents. Inozemtsev (1999; 1998a; 1998b; 1999; 2000) and Tsvylev (1997) are the most influential scholars of post-industrialism and information (knowledge) society. Both scholars have been educated in the Marxist tradition, which helped them develop an integral vision of global processes.

A growing number of Russian political scientists are working on developing a conceptual vision that goes beyond cleavage lines. They strive for a methodological renovation and a synthesis of the available approaches. A conscious effort in this respect has been undertaken by Vladislav Inozemtsev and myself. Early in 2000, we organized a two-day seminar outside of Moscow that brought together representatives of various research centers of globalization. Some of the papers presented at the seminar were collected in a book (Megatrendy 2001) that focused on the "mega-trends of global development." Methodologically, the book benefited from the evolutionary approach to globalization studies. A benefit of the approach is that various aspects, levels, and features of globalization are viewed in a more holistic and orderly perspective rather than as disjointed parts. To this effect, I have devised a conceptual model of chronopolitics, which uses "synchronizing" and "desynchronizing" dimensions to describe different trends of world development and views the emerging global reality as a "puff pastry," meaning a multi-layered structure of various evolutionary phenomena (Il'yin 1995a, b). A parallel conceptualization of world development has been suggested by Bogaturov and Voskresenski (1999). Their approach is complimentary to mine, and their idea of enclaves can be viewed as an alternative reproduction of Russian polity's evolutionary block structure (Il'yin 1995a).[13]

Despite these promising directions, Russian political science is still far from overcoming its divisions and parochialism. This is particularly true of political science at the university level, as many instructors continue to be committed to crude readings of cleavages—very much along the lines described in sections 2 and 3.

6. Studies of globalization effects on equity in Russian political science

The studies of globalization effects upon equity constitute an aspect of a broader research program on globalization. The fundamental *authority—people* cleavage provides wide room for such discussions. Scholars working in this tradition emphasize human resistance to centers of domination and therefore view globalization as detrimental to equity. Moral imperatives of equity make Boris Kapustin resist Fukuyama's "imperative of modernization," the "Washington consensus" of Williamson-Kolodko, and other ploys of globalists (Kapustin 2001b, 12). However morally justified and linked to emancipation of the oppressed, such a picture is one-dimensional and archaic. Universalistic moral and political claims are dismissive of not only transnational "rulers" of the world but also of any colleague trying to conduct more practically-oriented studies.

The *church—state* cleavage helps to identify plurality of national and civilizational situations. It also allows the revelation of some new varieties of equity. However, here the universalistic claims of moral political philosophers often tend to be replaced by particularistic claims of culture and civilization studies.

---

[13] The genealogy of the idea can be traced to the prismatic model (Riggs 1964).

Despite their contrasting conclusions, both schools of thought are similar. They present political actors as entangled in an epic struggle driven either by the mystics of the "clash of civilizations" or by the moral need to oppose "oppressive" globalization. One can guess that both ideas can be traced to the traditional Soviet emphasis on political struggle.

Very similar conclusions can be reached about works of leftist authors who associate globalization with various types of growing inequalities and injustices but rarely propose viable alternatives. The neo-Marxist search for alternatives to globalization is proving far more constructive. Thus, proponents of *alterglobalism* (Buzgalin 2003; Kagarlitski 2002) score a number of points by emphasizing the social creativity of protest movements against globalization. It is true that concerted efforts to achieve equity from below may prove effective. Yet the supporters of alterglobalism often ignore other alternatives. If all the alternatives are outside the process of globalization, what then is the nature of this broader global milieu? Who are the actors that shape this broader global setting of emerging reality? These questions suggest that the juxtaposition of globalization and alternatives initiated from below has its limitations.

In their turn, scholars working in the world-system tradition tend to argue the impossibility of achieving equity across the global *center—periphery* divide. Their resort to the *metropolis—colony* cleavage usually leads them to radical dependist or even apocalyptic conclusions about the future, such as "*tiersmondialization*" of the West, overpopulation, etc. (Volodin and Shirokov 2002, 208-212). On the other hand, Kondrat'ev's cycles and neo-institutionalism helps to identify contextual solutions to the emerging equity problems. This school believes that democratic practices and institutions may prove to be critical in achieving equity (Sergeyev 2001). As a result, globalization coupled with the recent wave of democratization may develop new forms of political pluralism (Mel'vil' 2003) and democracy (Il'yin 2003).

The need to diversify democracy and to develop adequate institutions and practices on the local levels is particularly important in the context of growing inequalities (Inozemtsev 2000). It turns out that, in addition to the traditional state and class divides, new divides have emerged, and cleavage analysis may assist us in identifying them. In this new global context, it is critical to reaffirm our understanding of democratic governance, justice, and equity. Currently, a group of researchers from MGIMO and IMEMO are engaged in a series of discussions, aimed at determining the evaluative standards of justice for various sectors of population and making them operational in the context of democratic governance. It is clear that such an ambitious goal cannot be reached without additional theoretical and empirical research. The evolutionary perspective of alternative developments, either multiple or enclave, may serve as a useful point of departure for such research, not just in Russia but also in other parts of the world.

7. Areas in need of more research in Russian political science

Further progress of Russian Political Science in the study of the interface between globalization and equity can only be accomplished by a sober turn to empirical research. Weakness of empirical research is currently a major handicap of political studies. Theoretical and descriptive aspects of the analysis still prevail in Russian political science, and researchers are only beginning to turn to empirical studies of globalization. In Russia, many aspects of globalization processes remain unexplored, some not even identified. Rare exceptions only emphasize this sad state of affairs. Thus, studies of global impact upon Russian regions might identify an important domain of future research. Comparative studies of institutions and practices seem particularly promising. Systematic comparative studies involving cases of other polities (India, South Africa etc.) would be particularly welcome. Russia, with its mixture of archaic, traditional, and modern institutions could also prove an excellent empirical terrain to study the effects of their interface with globalization.

References

Bogaturov, A. D. 1999. Sindrom pogloshcheniya v mirovoi politike. Pro et Contra 4.

Bogaturov, A. D. and A. V. Vinogradov. 1999. Model' ravnopolozhennogo razvitiya. Polis 4.

Buzgalin, A. V. 2001. Kontrgegemoniya i kontrglobalizatsiya. Al'ternativy 1.

Buzgalin, A. V. 2003. Al'terglobalizm kak fenomen sovremennogo mira. Polis 2.

Gorbachev, M., ed. 2002. Grani globalizatsii. Al'pina Press, Moskva.

Il'yin, M. V. 1995a. Ocherki khronopoliticheskoi tipologiyi. MGIMO, Moskva.

Il'yin, M. V. 1995b. Mirovoye obshcheniye kak problema "poliglotii." Polis 1.

Il'yin, M. V. 1997. Slova i smysl'y. ROSSPEN, Moskva.

Il'yin, M. V. 2003. Rossiyski vybor: sdelan, otsrochen, otmenen? Polis 2.

Ilyun, M. V. and V. L. Inozemtsev, eds. 2001. Megatrendy mirovogo razvitiya. A. M. Ekonomika, Moskva.

Inozemstev, V. L. 1995. K teorii postekonomicheskoi obshchestvennoi formatsiyi. Ekonomika, Moskva.

Inozemstev, V. L. 1998a. Za predelami ekonomicheskogo obshchestva. Moskva.

Inozemstev, V. L. 1998b. Za desyat' let. Moskva.

Inozemstev, V. L. 1999. Sotsial'no-ekonomicheskiye problemy XXI veka. Moskva.

Inozemstev, V. L. 2000. Tekhnologicheki progress i sotsial'naya polyarizatsiya v XXI stoletiyi. Polis 6.

Kagarlitski, B. 2002. Globalizatsiya i levyye. Moskva.

Kapustin, B. G. 2001a. Kritika politicheskogo moralizma. Voprosy filosofiyi 2.

Kapustin, B. G. 2001b. Konets «tranzitologii»? Polis 4.

Kollontai, V. 1999. O neoliberal'noi modeli globalizatsii. MEMO 10.

Kollontai, V. 2002. Evolyutsiya zapadnykh konsteptsiy globalizatsiyi. MEMO 1.

Lapkin, V. V. and V. I. Pantin. 1999. Geoekonomicheskaya politika. Polis 4.

Mel'vil', A. Yu., ed. 1997. Global'nyye sotsial'nyye i politicheskiye peremeny v mire. MGIMO, Moskva.

Mel'vil', A.Yu. 2003. O trayektoriyakh politicheskogo razvitiya postkommunisticheskikh stran. Polis 3.

Neklessa, A. I. 2000. Ordo Quadro—chetvertyi poryadok: prishestviye postsovremennogo mira. Polis 6.

Panarin, A. 1998. Revansh istorii. Logos, Moskva.

Panarin, A. 1999. Rossiya v tsyklakh mirovoi istoriyi. MGU, Moskva.

Panarin, A. 2000. Global'noye politicheskoye prognozirovaniye. Algoritm, Moskva.

Panarin, A. 2002. Iskusheniye globalizmom. Eksmo-press, Moskva.

Panarin, S. 2002. Pozitsionno-istoricheskiye faktory kavkazkoi politiki. Polis 2.

Pantin, V. I. 1997. Tsikly i volny modernizatsii kak fenomen sotsial'nogo razvitiya. Moskva.

Pantin, V. I. 2002. Vozmozhnosti tsiklicheski-volnovogo podkhoda k analizu politicheskogo razvitiya. Polis 4.

Pivovarov, Yu. S., A. I. Fursov. 2001. «Russkaya sistema» kak popytka ponimaniya russkoi istorii. Polis 4.

Popov, G. 2000. Globalizatsiya. Moskovski komsomolets, October.

Postindustrial'nyi mir: Tsentr, Periferiya i Rossiya. 1999. Vol. 1-4. MONF, IMEMO, Moskva.

Postindustrial'nyi mir i Rossiya. 2000. Editorial URSS, Moskva.

Riggs, F. W. 1957. Agraria and Industria. In: Toward a Comparative Study of Public Administration, edited by W.J. Siffin. Indiana University Press, Bloomington.

Riggs, F.W. 1964. Administration in Developing Countries. The Theory of Prismatic Society. Houghton Miffin. Boston.

Rokkan, S. 1959. Electoral Activity, Party Membership and Organizational Influence. Acta Sociologica 4.

Rokkan, S. and P. Torsvik. 1960. Der Waehler, der Leser und die Parteipresse. Koelner Zeitschrift fuer Soziologie 12.

Rokkan, S. 1966. Norway: Numerical Democracy and Corporate Pluralism. In: Political Oppositions in Western Democracies, edited by R. Dahl. Yale University Press, New Haven.

Rokkan, S. 1967. Geography, religion and Social Class. Cross-cutting Cleavages in Norwegian Politics. In: Party Systems and Voter Alignments, edited by S. M. Lipset and S. Rokkan. Free Press, New York.

Rokkan, S. and S. M. Lipset. 1967. Cleavage Structures, Party Systems and Voter Alignments. An Introduction. In: Party Systems and Voter Alignments, edited by S.M. Lipset and S. Rokkan. Free Press, New York.

Rokkan, S. 1968. Electoral Systems. In: International Encyclopedia of the Social Sciences. Free Press, New York.

Sergeyev, V. M. 2001. Vorota v global'nyi mir. In: Megatrendy mirovogo razvitiya, edited by M. V. Il'yin and V. L. Inozemtsev. Ekonomika, Moskva.

Tsvylev, R. I. 1997. Postindustrial'noye razvitiye: uroki dlya Rossii. Nauka, Moskva.

Veber, A. B. 2001. Predisloviye. In: Trudy Fonda Gorbacheva. Vol. 7. Problemy globalizatsii. Gorbachev-Fond, Moskva.

Volodin, A. G. and G. K. Shirokov. 1999. Globalizatsiya: istoki, tendentsii, perspektivy. Polis 5

Volodin, A. G. and G. K. Shirokov. 2002. Globalizatsiya: nachala, tendentsiyi, perspektivy. Moskva.

Yerasov, B. S. 2001. Sotsiokul'turnyye i geopoliticheskiye printsipy yevraziystva. Polis 5.

VI. Geopolitics in Russia—science or vocation?

Eduard G. Solovyev

1. Introduction

The main problem with Russian geopolitics is that it has not fully materialized as an academic discipline, though the academic programs have been established and a large number of textbooks published. In other words, although a geopolitical professional community has been formed in Russia, there is a deficit of some disciplinary norms and boundaries, which transform a branch of knowledge from an "art" or "craft" into an academic discipline. Russian national geopolitics lacks what defines any scientific discipline—the notions of professional competency and responsibility of geopoliticians as representatives of a certain academic community. Practically all independent geopolitical research is isolated from political theory and other social science disciplines. Methodological principles of geopolitics have not yet been clearly and consistently articulated. In a nutshell, there is too much of an "art" and too little of a "science" in geopoliticians' analyses, and personal experiences, talents, and authors' opinions continue to dominate the discipline. The present paper is an attempt to understand how and why this has happened.

2. Geopolitics in Russia: stages of development

This essay proposes a broad definition of geopolitics—as a system of ideas describing interrelationships between politics (world politics, above all) and the geographical environment, which translate into various forms of control over the space.

Development of geopolitical knowledge in our country has a relatively long history, spanning more than a century. Some adherents of modern Russian geopolitics are even inclined to trace the origins of this discipline to the principles of the Athenian democracy and see Aristotel as the founder of this "one of the most ancient political sciences" (Razuvayev 1993, 32). According to a widely held view, Russian geopolitical knowledge is nearly the earliest expression of public and political thought that emerged with the establishment of the ancient Russian state. However, statements about the geopolitical quality of a concept, such as "Moscow is the Third Rome," or about the existence of geopolitical thought in Russia in the pre-Mongol period (e.g. Kolosov and Mironenko 2002, 145-147; Kolosov 1996, 90-91; Trevish 1995) lack support. They attempt to modernize our ancestors' way of thinking. Geopolitics has developed along with political science and the concept of the modern state that includes sovereignty and defines territoriality as its key attributes. Russian early thinkers, such as Gostomysl' or Philofey, hardly thought in political categories of the modern state. The same can be said about geopolitical thinking attributed to the early XIX century Slavophiles and Westernizers, Nikolai Danilevski, Konstantin Leontyev, and other prominent Russian thinkers. Danilevski, for instance, was primarily interested in the special features and principal differences of Slavic and Roman-German cultures and civilizations. His main work (Danilevski 1998) is about the conflict of civilizations, rather than state-related geopolitical problems. The Slavophiles versus Westernizers debate was centered on the problem of Russia's choice of direction and pace of development. Work of a genuinely geopolitical emphasis emerged in Russia only in the late XIX-early XX centuries, in the works of Mechnikov (1995) and Semenov-Tyanshanski (1915), and in the theories of the Eurasianists (see especially Savitski 1997).

Semenov-Tyanshanski, in particular, tried to make sense of various forms of "territorial systems of political might." He was quite original in his arguments and did not follow the questionable concepts of British geopolitics, which operated within the dichotomy of Land- and Sea-based powers and assumed the eternal conflict of the so-called "Tellourocratic" and "Talassocratic" nations. Writing about spatial and territorial characteristics of the world's leading nations, Semenov-Tyanshanski described them as having attributes of geographical linkages, territorial concentration, and "sea to sea" connections. For the Russian empire, he saw the principal means of strengthening unity and power in developing a special cultural and economic region between the Volga and Yenisei rivers. The idea of such a region becoming the new political and geographical center of the country was further developed during the 1990s in the works of Tsymburski (1995, 1999).

As for Eurasianism, this geopolitical movement was born among Russian émigrés in the 1920s and lasted until the World War II. It presented arguments about Russia's harmony and uniqueness as a special world combining the elements of both Europe and Asia, with the latter predominating. It also insisted on Russia's economic and cultural self-sufficiency. To the Eurasianists, Russia was to be seen as a "middle continent" (Eurasia), rather than as a land divided between Europe and Asia. By Asia, they meant China, India, Iran, and other territories, whereas Europe was perceived to reach from its western boundaries to the eastern border of Poland and Romania. In such interpretation, the middle continent was also a cultural melting pot for Slavic and Turkish peoples, which formed the organic nature of Russian Eurasian ethnicity and culture.

Despite their conservatism, the ideas of Eurasinists did not find support in the Soviet Union, in part because of the official taboo against the very notion of geopolitics. One might, of course, reflect about the geopolitical aspects of Stalin's concept of the "spheres of interest," which underlay the specifics of the Yalta-Potsdam system of international relations. Or about the "Brezhnev's doctrine," which limited the sovereignty of the Warsaw Pact countries and was designed to preserve the Soviet sphere of influence in Europe. Yet conscious geopolitical thinking was hardly behind these foreign policy doctrines. Rather, these doctrines were permeated by the philosophy of *realpolitik* and were constructed in the spirit of traditional imperialism.

Discussions about the need to develop a "Soviet geopolitical theory" (the expression is believed to belong to Georgi Shakhnazarov) emerged in Russia only in the 1970s. However, even at that time the discussion did not go very far since, in the Soviet public mind, geopolitics was too closely associated with the names of Karl Haushofer and other supporters of Nazi Germany's doctrine of the "Third Reich." It was viewed as a form of reactionary ideology, designed to justify the expansionist foreign policy of the West. Only in the 1970-1980s did some serious studies devoted to development of geo-strategy and geopolitical analysis begin to appear in Russia (Lukin 1983; Ponomareva and Smirnova

1986). As for the idea of developing a Soviet geopolitical theory, it was completely abandoned.

3. The rise of geopolitics after the Soviet breakup

The disintegration of the USSR and the new policy of Perestroika were followed by a boom of geopolitics in Russia. Neglected for so many years, the discipline was now viewed as having answers to the new challenges in international relations presented by the changes of the 1980-1990s. The social and ideological context of the late Perestroika and the following dissolution of the Soviet Union played an important role in the process. The public, accustomed to the Marxist-Leninist claims of absolute truth, could not quite accept the seemingly sudden breakup of the system and was ready to turn to a new "genuinely truthful" and "scientific" ideology for explanation. However, many modern social sciences, including critical geopolitics, operated with only relative and probabilistic notions and could hardly offer any ultimate judgments. It is in this context that so many found it appealing to turn to the essentialist and highly deterministic theories of traditional geopolitics, as developed in the early-mid XX century by Halford Mackinder, Nickolas Spykmann, Karl Haushofer, and others.

Traditional geopolitics studies states as spatial and political phenomena. Their main emphasis is on power, and its research goals are to understand the causes of the rise and fall of state power in international relations. This is why some authors characterized geopolitics as a branch of political realism (Tsygankov 1996, 157). Yet, traditional geopolitics, relative to realism, is often even more reductionist in putting almost exclusive emphasis on state size and geography in explaining state behavior and in searching solutions to world problems. The state emerges as a spatial and territorial organism with its own physical resources: climate, landscape, flora, soil, geology, transport communications and, above all, geographical location are seen to determine the main objectives of state foreign policy and opportunities for its implementation.

However, it is this reductionism, simplicity, and the claimed ability to provide clear and (within the frames of traditional geographical determinism) unambiguous answers to complicated questions of the modern world that has drawn a

wide array of post-Soviet Russian scholars and politicians to traditional geopolitics. Geopolitics in Russia claims solutions to some ultimate puzzles in global politics, offering both mystical and deterministic explanations for current
and future events. The concept of controlled or mastered space was presented as the inevitable and ultimate foundation of world order. Geopolitics
became the mirror image of Mikhail Gorbachev's political idealism and Yeltsin-
Kozyrev's political subservience and non-stop concessions to the West.

Another aspect of geopolitics' popularity in Russia has to do with the ideological demand for it. The reductionism of geographical determinism created
an opportunity to use geopolitics as an ideological motivation and ideological
justification of foreign policy priorities. Unexpectedly, geopolitics in Russia has
demonstrated its mobilization potential and ability to influence large audiences. In this sense, it went far beyond a scientific discipline and turned into a
"scientifically justified doctrine" and the ultimate ideological replacement for
Marxism-Leninism. As the result, geopolitical terminology is now being used
by both state officials and the representatives of the opposition. Geopolitical
reasoning is behind such issues as Russia's non-membership in European
institutions and its often tense relationship with the United States. Geopolitical
considerations played a key role in the perception of relations with NATO, in
the evaluation of prospects for integration with the Newly Independent States,
in the building of ties with China and India, the designing of the "multipolar
world" doctrine, and so on. Geopolitics influences, directly or indirectly, the formation and implementation of Russia's foreign policy strategy.

Finally, the appeal of geopolitics to Russia's extreme right and left can be
explained by its correlation to some persistent and long established stereo-
types of their political conscience. This means the idea of eternal and inevitable confrontation between Russia and the West, or the necessity of Russia's
military and political self-sufficiency in order to survive in the constantly threat-
ening environment. Over the past decade, far right political thought has developed different variations of geopolitical imagination about the past, present,
and future of Russia and the world order (Zhirinovski 1996; Mitrofanov 1997).
Works of the leader of the Communist Party of Russian Federation (CPRF)
Gennadi Zyuganov (1995, 1998) also considerably contributed to the development of geopolitical thinking in the country. Communist geopolitics empha-

sizes such notions as "*derzhava*" (Great Power from Russian "power holder"), "socialism," and "Russian statehood." The communists present Russia's long history as a coherent and continuous process by drawing a straight line between the XVth century projects of "gathering Russian lands" to the CPRF calls for a revival of the Soviet empire. The communists view the relationship between Russia and the West in primarily confrontational terms and insist that Russia must resist the unipolar trends in global politics, viewed as the "dictatorship of the US and NATO" (Zyuganov 1998, 243). The hard-core geopolitical vision of the world has also made possible the so-called synthesis of the radical right and left, uniting "red" and "white" nationalists on the platform of opposing Yeltsin's status quo.

However, present world realities are much too complicated to be convincingly analyzed through the methods of traditional geopolitics. Geopolitics as a discipline certainly cannot afford to ignore the problems of territory, location, and ethnicity of a nation. But it also cannot abstract from some qualitatively new transformations taking place in the world arena. In the 1990s, many Russian scholars (Gadzhiyev 1998; Sorokin 1996; Smirnov 1999; Solovyev 2001) developed a clear understanding that the traditional models required serious correction. The development of military technologies, the collapse of bipolarity, and the formation of a new world order do not only mean the emergence of a new geopolitical reality as determined by change in the old balance of power. Nor is it merely a complication of the old geopolitical structure of the world stemming from the growing power of regions outside the United States and Russia. What we are witnessing is how the mutual relations of power centers, regions, and individual states obtain a new complex and multi-dimensional quality and how the previously clear boundaries are disappearing. A number of parameters defining the world politics have increased, whereas economic, military, spatial, and geographical forms of domination have further diversified. State and non-state actors are increasingly finding new and divergent areas of political control, and the very parameters of statehood and world hegemony are being actively rethought. It becomes obvious, as never before, that geopolitics deals not with constants or reality "as we know it," but rather with social and humanitarian phenomena, which can be interpreted and reinterpreted by various researchers in various ways.

Realization of all these problems urged the revision and rethinking of traditional geopolitical concepts. Along with the noted flaws of the traditional geopolitical analysis, the transformation of Western geopolitical research made a significant impact upon the intellectual atmosphere and discussions in Russia. Western authors, supportive of so-called "critical geopolitics," have transformed the old geopolitical knowledge to fit the modern realities and now identify several new research areas for geopolitics. These areas include "formal geopolitics," which studies and critically reflects on the development of geopolitical thought and tradition, "practical geopolitics," which concentrates on mass geographical symbols, images and ideas, as well as on their social interpretations and projections to the world, and "structural geopolitics," which studies, above all, the impact of globalization and informatization, the realities of public risk, and the transformation geopolitical practices (Agnew 1994; O Tuathail 1996, 1999, 2000).

4. The principal schools of modern Russian geopolitics

The development of geopolitical knowledge in Russia went in at least two major directions. The first school of thought is a synthesis of the traditional Western geopolitical concepts and Russian Eurasianism. The second school is a response to the need for fundamental rethinking of the old theoretical synthesis.

Neo-Eurasianism: The specifics of geopolitical approaches

In the 1990s, Eurasianism reemerged and developed several new versions. The magazine *Elementy* and newspaper *Zavtra* (formerly, *Den'*) became the main advocates of Neo-Eurasianism in the mass media and Dugin (1998) emerged as its primary theorist. Panarin (1995, 2000a) and some other authors developed their own alternative versions of Neo-Eurasianism.

Students and followers of Dugin view geopolitics as a universal science that possesses the knowledge of the laws and the spiritual and cultural determinants of international relations. In their turn, the ideologists of Neo-Eurasianism do their best to make their findings accessible to a broad audience by trying to operate with the notions and archetypes reminiscent of the Soviet thinking. For example, in his pragmatic work *Foundations of Geopolitics*, Dugin (1998, 7) asserts that Marxism comes the closest to Geopolitics in terms of its universality and methodological rigor:

> Marxist analysis is equally important for both the forces of Capital and for the fighters for emancipation of Labor. The same applies to Geopolitics—it teaches large states (imperia) how to best maintain territorial hegemony and to continue to expand. The opponents, however, also find this theory useful for learning about their self-protection and "national redemption."

For Dugin, geopolitics is a "synthetic" scientific discipline that incorporates the elements of geography, history, demography, strategy, ethnography, theology, ecology, sociology, political science and so on—in other words, not a discipline, but a system of disciplines united by a world outlook. Marxism and liberalism are viewed as analogies to geopolitics.

Dugin's supporters believe that configurations of world politics are defined by the principal dualism and confrontation of sea-based and land-based empires. The land-based power is directly associated with attachment to a particular space and cultivation of stability of its main quality characteristics. In a cultural or civilizational sense, it practices values of conservatism, non-migration, austerity, tradition, and the invariability of judicial and ethic norms. The peoples of Land power value collectivism and hierarchy and do not have much regard for individualism and entrepreneurship. The sea-based power is the opposite cultural and civilizational type. "Sea civilizations" are adaptable, dynamic, and are open to social and technological innovations. On the high priority list of this cultural and civilizational type have always been sailing and trade, which reflected its social individualism and the so-called "spirit of entrepreneurship." The two civilizations—Eurasianism versus Atlanticism—are fundamentally irreconcilable although the degree of their confrontation and balance of power may vary from one historical period to another.

Panarin (1999, 2000a) offers a more philosophically and politically refined interpretation of Neo-Eurasianism. In his views, "the Eurasianist project seeks to find a solution to two central tasks: how to restore the wholeness of the post-Soviet space and how to revive the spirit of Russia" (Panarin 1995, 66). After the collapse of the "Second World," Russia is facing the choice of either restoring its lost "big space" by spiritually, morally, economically and techno- logically transforming it, or becoming a part of the "Third World" and loosing any sense of perspective forever. Obviously, put in such a way, Russia has only one choice and that is to restore the former USSR.

The dualism of "land" and "sea" is also fundamental for Panarin's theory. Under his authorship, the Land becomes a symbol of everything solid and sta- ble (Panarin 2000b, 326), whereas the Sea civilizations are designated as products of "global pirates" (2000b, 376). The primary objective for Panarin, however, is not to "return" the former Russian territories or to unite the Eur- asian space under Russia's leadership. The key task is to transform the unipo- lar world order into something else, either a multipolar or a bipolar structure. It is the restoration of the system of checks and balances on the world scale and the prevention of a purely hegemonic model of world order that Panarin views as Russia's main objective. While not sharing Dugin's somewhat mystical vision of Eurasia, Panarin believes in constructing scenarios of the world's development or "futurist projects" for the purpose of achieving the identified objective. In his "futurist project," Russia develops multilateral contacts with India, China, and the Muslim states in order to restore its power and to under- mine Western global hegemony (Panarin 2002, 45-51).

Geopolitical revisionism

In the early-mid 1990s, Russian scholars made the first steps towards a trans- formation of the subject of geopolitical research. For example, Pleshakov (1994a) argued that in order to survive as a branch of knowledge, geopolitics had to adapt to changes while preserving the coherence of its subject. In his view, geopolitics should continue to study control over space, but acknowledge that the forms of this control—military, political, civilizational, communicational, demographic, and so on—have been transformed significantly. Pleshakov's other innovation (1994b) was to examine the problems of geopolitics in the context of evolving political ideologies. The proposed framework applies well to some geopolitical developments of the past, such as the Cold War, but does not seem to have much to offer for understanding the present and the future.

Tsymburski's (1995) contribution was in offering an original interpretation of Russia as a geopolitical "island." It implied that despite some principal geographical changes over the centuries, the Russian territory has established the core of its stability. That core is away from the European part of Russia, and post-Soviet Russia should do well to shift power to the Ural Mountains and Siberia. Tsymburski is also known in Russia as a supporter for moving the Russian capital from Moscow to the city of Novosibirsk in Siberia. He is also known for his scholarship on large historical cycles of Russian geopolitical practices (Tsymburski 1996), in which he attempts to trace the impact of 150 years-long military cycles on world developments.[1]

Sorokin (1996) went further and proposed relinquishing the "politico-spatial thinking" of traditional Western geopolitics since it was unable to adequately respond to contemporary challenges. His solution was not to cling to the traditional subject of geopolitics, but rather to expand it radically and to develop a discipline that would study "multi-layered and multi-level global politics," as well as the "multi-dimensional and multi-polar world" (Sorokin 1996, 16).

Gadzhiyev (1995) developed this line of thinking by proposing associating geopolitics with the study of the evolution and transformation of the world order, including the modern world order. Gadzhiyev identifies the key problems for current geopolitical analysis as the structure of a new world order (unipolarity vs. multipolarity), dimensions of the power allocation, and the process of formation of a common global community. In this case, the prefix geo- refers to the global ambitions of the discipline, rather than to its traditional geographical focus. This represents a far reaching re-structuring of geopolitics that in the future is intended to study overlaps of international, transnational, and global characteristics in the modern world community. It is associated with the structures, strategic directions, laws and principles of the functioning and evolving modern world community. In such an interpretation, geopolitics gains a new meaning and opens itself to collaboration with other disciplines, such as inter-

---

[1] Panarin also undertook a similar effort (1999) by placing Russia's development in the context of world historical cycles.

national relations, international law, political science, cultural studies, and others. As a result, geopolitics presents itself as the framework for integrating various branches of social and humanitarian knowledge. It becomes a complex social discipline with emphasis on multiple expressions of the modern world.

Along these lines, some scholars have proposed to view geopolitics as part of political geography, defining geopolitics as study of the state in the context of international affairs (Kolosov 1992; Turovski 1999; Kolosov and Mironenko 2002). For example, Kolosov develops the notion of geopolitics of cooperation, which (1) emphasizes communication between spatial systems, not just conflicts between them; (2) studies new forms of political activism in the world arena (transnational business, non-governmental organizations, separatist movements and so on); and (3) studies aspects of global geopolitical interdependence and their expressions, such as socio-economic and ecological crises (Kolosov 1992; Kolosov and Mironenko 2002, 170-172).

Zamyatin's work (1998, 2001a, b) is yet another very interesting direction of geopolitical reflection, influenced by the methods and theories of Western critical geopolitics. Zamyatin views geopolitics as a discipline with major tasks in allocating power and influencing society through the creation and projection of geopolitical images. As a result, geopolitical images may acquire different forms, depending upon the goals and resources of their creators. At the same time, images remain open to interpretation and reinterpretation. In such a presentation, geopolitics emerges not as a projection of a geographical map, but rather as an active participant in a map-making processes. Rather than being "natural," geopolitics becomes the subject to critical construction in the interest of achieving certain political objectives (Lurye and Kazaryan 1994; Zamyatin 1998, 2001a, b).

In addition, financial globalization and the informational revolution have stimulated the development of geo-economics as a special, if not the most important, form of geopolitical projection (Sorokin 1996; Kochetov 1997, 1999). Under the new global conditions, economic conflicts emerge as the key source of potential international hostilities. Many scholars caution about the possible coming of *realekonomik* era, which will see as its essence fierce economic competition and even confrontation among territorially confined units (Kochetov 1999).

5. The Future of Russian geopolitics

The revisionist geopolitical theories presented Russian scholarly community with an elaborate alternative vision and outlined promising new directions for research. They have also revealed some serious problems and limitations of methodological nature. First and foremost, the increase in the level of "complexity," for which many scholars of geopolitics have called, potentially creates new problems. At some point, every scholar is faced with the methodological necessity of either simplifying a theoretical framework by taking into consideration only those factors that matter the most or undermining the clarity and cohesiveness of disciplinary boundaries. Viewed in this light, the complexity of the discipline may be a questionable blessing. Although Sorokin (1996) and some other revisionists are correct to note the growing complexity of the global order, the real picture includes elements of both new and old trends and leaves sufficient room for both conflict and cooperation in the world. So long as this is the case, there is also room for traditional geopolitics with its emphasis on principal contradictions among spatial units.

On the other hand, merging geopolitics with the fields of ethnic studies, political science, international relations, or others is likely to result in overloading geopolitics with new problems like excessively broad generalizations, rather than genuinely enriching it with new methods and research strategies. In the meantime, if we are to call things by their name, modern geopolitics, while struggling to preserve its ontological status of a scientific discipline, is on its way to turning into a kind of political philosophy. It is turning into what might be called a philosophy of international relations or foreign policy, which is either overloaded by normative judgments or suffers from some "naïve Machiavellianism." While the revisionists tend to operate with normative generalities, such as a "multi-layer" and "multi-dimensional" world (Sorokin 1996), traditionalists openly offer themselves to the elite as providers of the "art of ruling" (Dugin 1998). All discussions about creating a principally new complex scientific discipline of geopolitics remain no more than that. Various scholars, often independently of each other, argue the importance of revising traditional geopolitics, but are unable to offer a coherent vision in this regard. Perhaps, a switch from the highly theoretical discussion about world order to case-studies of regional and trans-regional allocation of powers or even "micro"-geopolitical analyses will assist us in better defining the disciplinary boundaries and getting closer to solving some pressing methodological problems.[2]

Another methodological problem of geopolitics is its persistent state-centrism. Although it is true that the state remains the only legitimate and fully sovereign political actor on the global scene, it is also true that overemphasis on the state may make it impossible to adequately assess the role of actors without sovereignty, such as various national and international organizations, associations, firms, transnational groups, etc. These actors might and should be studied in their own right, not exclusively, but so long as they are related to the activities of some powerful states. Even more inadequate is the assumption of state-centrism in geo-economics. Globalization of finances and information promoted geo-economics to the status of a most important branch of geopolitics, as many scholars noted (Sorokin 1996; Kochetov 1997; Jan and Savona 1997). Geo-economics should study flows, regulation and management of various resources across the globe. Yet in practice, it focuses too often on the strategy of achieving state interests under the conditions of economic globalization (Kochetov 1999). International interdependence is often studied solely in its applied meaning. Meanwhile, a situation where the U.S. lobbies Japanese business interests in Europe because they produce their automobiles at American plants or other such collisions and conflicts remain outside the sphere of analysis of modern geo-economics.

The practical orientation of geopolitics—its special characteristics—only exacerbates the problem, as researchers develop their taste for providing advice to the powerful of this world. In this situation, the most reasonable thing to do would be to gain some distance from the attempts to produce effective geo-strategic projects and to return to the attempts of understanding the nature of geopolitics as an academic discipline. If it is a science or has scientific elements, it should have its own subject and methods of analysis.

Finally, it is time for Russian geopolitics to become less Russia-centric, as the focus of Russian geopolitical reflection is undoubtedly on the role and place of Russia in Eurasia. As Kolosov and Turovski (2000, 22) write, the

---

[2] Certain steps in this direction are already being made (Gadzhiyev 2001).

assumption of Russo-centrism has created a false image of Russia "as the key to global stability and the geographical center of world politics," as well as some idealized perceptions of Russia's geopolitical mission. Russia as the strategic axis of Eurasia is a myth; Russia may be, as some have argued, not the world's geopolitical axis, but a "geopolitical dead-end." (Turovski 1994, 31; 1995).

Further development of Russian geopolitics would benefit from a dialogue among several of the above identified schools and approaches. One of them views geopolitics as a complex scientific discipline, and it is the closest to a philosophy of foreign policy and international relations. Another school tends to interpret geopolitics as a branch of a broader discipline, political geography. Still another school defends the notion of a fundamental dualism of political societies (Neo-Eurasianism). Up until now, none of these schools have expressed either readiness or willingness to lead an open discussion on a broad spectrum of geopolitical problems. Yet, it is in such a discussion that Russian geopolitics would eventually be able to define itself as a vocation and as an academic discipline.

References

Agnew, J. A. 1994. The Territorial Gap: The Geographical Assumptions of International Relations Theory. Review of International Political Economy 1 (1).

Danilevski, N. 1998. Rossiya i Yevropa. Arktogeya, Moskva.

Dugin, A. 1998. Osnovy geopolitiki. Arktogeya, Moskva.

Gadzhiev, K. S. 1995. Geopolitika: istoriya i sovremennoye soderzhaniye distsipliny. Polis 4.

Gadzhiev, K. S. 1998. Geopolitika. Yuniti, Moskva.

Gadzhiev, K. S. 2001. Geopolitika Kavkaza. Mezhdunarodnyye otnosheniya, Moskva.

Jan, K. and P. Savona. 1997. Geoekonomika. Mezhdunarodnyye otnosheniya, Moskva.

Kochetov, E. 1997. Geoekonomika i strategiya Rossii. Ekonomika, Moskva.

Kochetov, E. 1999. Geoekonomika. Ekonomika, Moskva.

Kolosov, V. A. 1992. Territorial'no-politicheskaya organizatsiya obshchestva. Moskva.

Kolosov, V. A. 1996. Rossiyskaya geopolitika: traditsionnye kontseptsii i sovremennye vyzovy. Obshchestvennyye nauki i sovremennost' 3.

Kolosov, V. A. and S. Turovski, eds. 2000. Geopoliticheskoe polozhenie Rossii: predstavleniya i realnost'. No publisher information, Moskva.

Kolosov, V. A. and N. S. Mironenko. 2002. Geopolitika i politicheskaya geographiya. Aspekt press, Moskva.

Lukin, V.P. 1983. "Tsentry sily": kontseptsii i realnost'. Nauka, Moskva.

Lurie, S. and L. Kazaryan. 1994. Printsipy organizatsii geopoliticheskogo prostranstva. Obshchestvennye nauki i sovremennost' 4.

Mechnikov, L. 1995. Tsivilizatsiya i velikiye istoricheskiye reki. No publisher information, Moskva.

Mitrofanov, A. 1997. Shagi novoi geopolitiki. No publisher information, Moskva.

O Tuathail, G. 1996. Critical Geopolitics: The Politics of Writing Global Space. University of Minnesota Press, Minneapolis.

O Tuathail, G. 1999. Understanding Critical Geopolitics: Geopolitics and Risk Security. The Journal of Strategic Studies 22 (2-3).

O Tuathail, G. 2000. Geopolitics in a Changing World. New York.

Panarin, A. S. 1995. Evraziyski proyekt v mirosystemnom kontekste. Vostok 2.

Panarin, A. S. 1999. Rossiya v tsiklakh mirovoi istoriyi. MGU, Moskva.

Panarin, A. S. 2000a. Iskusheniye globalizmom. Algoritm, Moskva.

Panarin, A. S. 2000b. Politologiya. Gadrarika, Moskva.

Panarin, A. S. 2002. Ontologiya terrora. In: Geopolitika terrora. Moskva.

Pleshakov, K. 1994a. Geopolitika v svete global'nykh peremen. Mezhdunarodnaya zhizn' 10.

Pleshakov, K. 1994b. Geo-ideologicheskaya paradigma. No publisher information, Moskva.

Ponomareva, I. B. and N. A. Smirnova. 1986. Geopolitika imperializma Soedinennykh Shtatov Ameriki. Nauka, Moskva.

Razuvaev, V. V. 1993. O ponyatiyi "Geopolitika." Vestnik MGU: Sotsial'no-politicheskiye issledovaniya 4.

Savitski, P. N. 1997. Kontinent Yevraziya. Agraf, Moskva.

Semenov-Tyanshanski, V. 1915. O mogushchestvennom territorial'nom vladenii primenitel'no k Rossii. Peterburg.

Smirnov, A. N. 1999. Urovni geopoliticheskogo vospriyatiya deistvitelnosti v sovremennoi Rossiyi. Vestnik MGU: Politicheskiye nauki 3.

Solovyev, E. G. 2001. Geopoliticheskiy analiz mezhdunarodnykh problem sovremennosti. Pro et Contra 6.

Sorokin, K. E. 1996. Geopolitika sovremennosti i geostrategiya Rossii. MNF, Moskva.

Trevish, A. 1995. Rossiyskaya geopolitika ot Gostomysl'a do nashikh dnei. Znanie-Sila 5.

Tsygankov, P. A. 1996. Mezhdunarodnye otnoshniya. Vysshaya shkola, Moskva.

Tsymburski, V. L. 1995. Zauralski Peterburg: alternativa dlya rossiskoi tsivilizatsiyi. Biznes i politika 1.

Tsymburski, V. L. 1996. Sverkhdlinnyye voennyye tsikly novogo i noveishego vremeni. Polis 3.

Tsymburski, V. L. 1999. Geopolitika dlya "yevraziyskoi Atlantidy." Pro et Contra 4 (4).

Turovski, R. F. 1994. Politiko-geographicheskoye polozheniye Rossii i interesy gosudarstva. Kentavr 3.

Turovski, R. F. 1995. Yadro Evrazii ili eye tupik? In: Rossiya na novom rubezhe, Moskva.

Turovski, R. F. 1999. Politicheskaya geographiya. Moskva, Smolensk.

Zamyatin, D. N. 1998. Politiko-geograficheskiye obrazy i geopoliticheskiye kartiny mira. Polis 6.

Zamyatin, D. N. 2001a. Geograficheskie obrazy mirovogo razvitiya. Obshchestvennye nauki i sovremennost' 1.

Zamyatin, D. N. 2001b. Geopolitika: osnovnyye problemy i itogi razvitiya v XX veke. Polis 6.

Zhirinovski, V. V. 1996. Posledniy brosok na Yug. In: V. V. Zhirinovski, Politicheskaya klassika. Vol. 6, No publisher information, Moskva.

Zyuganov, G. A. 1995. Za gorizontom. No publisher information, Moskva.

Zyuganov, G. A. 1998. Geografiya pobedy. No publisher information, Moskva.

VII. Ethnicity and the study of international relations in the post-Soviet Russia

By Nayil' M. Mukharyamov

1. Introduction

Russian approaches to the study of ethnicity in international relations have their own specifics that might be explained by dramatic events of the country's recent history. These include: radical changes in its geopolitical status, new ethno-political factors that emerged in the aftermath of the Soviet breakup, and the society's "identity crisis." Discussions of ethno-national and ethno-political issues by international relations scholars are therefore taking place in Russia against the backdrop of a fragmented and deeply divided society. Often, these discussions become extremely heated and politicized, making it impossible to continue exchanges of opinions, let alone reaching some sort of an agreement. In some cases, such discussions take personal turns, as participants question not only epistemological and theoretical positions of opponents, but also their professional competence. Despite these difficulties, theoretical debates in Russia have progressed and produced some interesting and productive ways of responding to new realities. As tentative as it can be, this essay outlines several dominating tendencies and themes in Russian analysis of ethnicity. It examines some innovative approaches to the nature of ethnicity and its role in the formation of world order after the Cold War. It also analyzes the issues of ethnic identity formation and ethnic conflicts in the works of Russian researches.

2. Main theoretical approaches to ethnicity in international relations

It is hard to identify theoretical and methodological positions of Russian political scientists in discussions of ethnicity in international relations and foreign policy. Yet, one could tentatively outline two main perspectives on the role of ethnonational factors in world order: substantialism and instrumentalism or relationism.

Substantialism views the ethnonational and ethnopolitical aspects as indispensable attributes of the system of international relations and foreign policy. To substantialists, ethnicity is a driving force behind international decisions and practical actions. The supporters of this approach take a state-centric view, assuming that state behavior in the arena of world politics is also defined primarily by ethnonational considerations. States are the main, and probably the only, significant actors in international affairs. Such a view is reminiscent of the Soviet-era class reductionism, with the only difference being that ethnicity is now elevated to the position of representing the "Truth" in world politics.

Another feature of substantialism is to view ethnic groups as fundamental subjects of international relations and international law, entitled to the protection of their rights, rather than as actors who sporadically appear on the world political scene to challenge the existing order. In this respect, substantialists are similar to gender scholars of nationalism who often treat nations as individuals or acting personalities of history, each with their character, soul, mission, will power, and "life cycles including birth, periods of adolescence and aging, and a fear of death, [with]…territories as their material references, not unlike the human body" (Verderi 2002, 300).

These two features or trends seem contradictory and unrealistic. Indeed, what could be common between the supporters of ethnonational separatism and state unitarism that rejects the very possibility of minority groups having an independent subjectivity? From our point of view, the way to combine these two features is in acknowledging the principal primacy of ethnonational substance in the system of social relations, including international political relations. In this respect, it is symptomatic that substantialists commonly share an admiration for scholarship of Lev N. Gumilev. For instance, it is in reference to Gumilev's essentialist views of ethnicity that Yuri P. Platonov (2002, 11) writes: "The ethnoses are the main actors of history because they represent the most stable and active human entities, comprising all people; there is no man without an ethnos and every man belongs to only one ethnos."

Those sharing the substantialist approach tend to unite geopolitics and ethnopolitics into a single conceptual complex. Yuri M. Borodai (1995) can be considered a pioneer in rethinking geopolitics in ethnonational categories. In his view:

> Ideas about *national* geopolitics have little in common with prominent doctrines, designed to formulate and justify the principles of state foreign policy, and the methods and directions of state *imperial* expansion. These currently popular classical geopolitics owe their development in the West to the founder of political geography Ratzel, the British geographer Mackinder, the German Haushofer, the American Spikeman, and others. In practice, however, geopolitics does not take into consideration the problem of *ethnic compatibility*. Yet, unlike such popular imperialist doctrines based upon geography, the fundamentals of national geopolitics must be based upon *ethnography*. (Borodai 1995, 130-131)

Borodai proposes to examine the problem of borders not only in the politico-territorial, interstate dimension, which does not always match the national dimension. He shifts the attention to the spiritual and ethical compatibility and complementarity, and raises the questions about ethnicities' need to get along with each other and act together, sharing some common moral dominants. "National borders are meant to unite what is compatible—at least in the foreseeable future. This is the essence of the *ethno-geopolitical* approach" (emphasis is added—N.M.) (Borodai 1995).

In Russia's contemporary literature, the ethno-geopolitical approach has been relatively well established. Following Gumilev and Borodai, the already cited Platonov (2002, 399) attributes to the "ethnic actor" such characteristics as determination, motivation, structure, coherence, integrity, organization, will, and the "existence in time and space." He considers social orientations of ethnic actors an integral factor in ethnic collective interaction.

The outlined approach has its implications for foreign policy and the theory of International Relations. Its supporters define geopolitics as a science of "geographic determination of ethno-political processes in the domestic arena and in international relations" (Platonov 2002, 492). The approach also serves to justify the so-called Russia-centrism as a foreign policy ideology and geopolitical orientation. To the advocates of the approach, it is an important one, as:

in the opinion of the majority of Russian specialists, geopolitics must operate not only with categories of the state but also with those of culture and ethnicity and, especially, with how they apply to categories of "statehood," "nation," "spirituality," and "ethnic complementarity" (Platonov 2002, 241).

The well-known communist politician Ilyukhin (1999) also insisted that acknowledging the nation as a subject of historical processes must be the core of the national security concept and of any analysis of problems of "security in general and national (ethnic) security in particular." The official or presidential concept of national security, he charged, "ignores the ethnicity" and, as a result, "anti-historical" and "anti-national" initiatives and political practices will be likely to continue (Ilyukhin 1999, 28, 66). Therefore, in regard to policy, the core of the substantialist approach is also in combining geopolitics and ethnopolitics in moving historical processes.

An alternative approach attempts to combine substantionalist and activity-based aspects in the ethnicity concept. Belkov, for instance, proposed one such interpretation by emphasizing that ethnicity is not only of substantive nature. It also has an important functional attribute: it is able to become a driving force in history when actively supported and promoted politically (2001, 291). Sharing his thoughts about the "ethnification of politics and polarization of ethnicity," Belkov concludes that "political will in solving ethnopolitical problems, as well as avoidance of decisions, makes a significant, often defining impact on all aspects of life of individual countries and the world as a whole" (2001, 292).

The *instrumentalist* or relationist approach builds upon ideas that go beyond substantialism's essentialist categories and rejects the very principles of substantialism. The pluralism of ideas and methodology that came to Russian political science along with political changes of the late 1980s—early 1990s contributed greatly to the division between substantialists and instrumentalists. The non-substantialist way of thinking about history began to spread and to challenge substantialism. It is defined by Pivovarov (2002) as a way of thinking according to which:

final responsibility for events and actions ultimately lies with a force of historical necessity. An individual or personality in the frame of such approaches is but an expression of some higher values and—in the long run—is merely a part of some hierarchically organized whole entity (Ibid, 92).

A different approach was coming to replace the emphasis on politics centered on nations or large social groups (peoples, masses, classes, etc.) that had been common for the Soviet official ideological routine and professional academic discourse. The new approach wanted to examine the context of political action and rejected the principle of assigning ontological status to ethnicity. The supporters of this approach proclaimed: "By its nature the ethnos is not a subject of politics, but rather is a context of an individual's cultural belongingness" (Guseinov, Dragunski, Sergeyev, and Tsymburski 1990, 17). By this they aimed to de-ethnicize national politics and de-politicize ethnonational relations.

The studies of ethnicity came under expanding influence of sociological constructivism. The latter was expressed in the "historical-situational" method offered by Valeri Tishkov (1997) as a challenge to the essentialist or substantialist tradition of understanding ethnicity as a political force. Along with others, Tishkov understood ethnic identity to be socially constructed and therefore relative, rather than essentialist, in its nature. He underscored the need to understand the notion of identity for understanding the nature of ethnicity. To him, identity was a competitive and pluralistic entity that was constantly in the process of construction and a "result of dialogue and relations among different social groups, between the state and a group, and between different states" (Tishkov 1997, 63).

The ethno-political *problematique* in Russian international relations increasingly began to reflect the relationist understanding. Scholars viewed ethnicity not as a result of interaction between some ontologically real and homogeneous social subjects (driving forces or acting personalities of history). To them, it is a product of a complex interaction among various actors—elite, state bureaucracy, agents of mass communication, and intellectuals—and their political activities. The following thesis of Tishkov can well summarize the motto of methodological instrumentalism in understanding ethnicity: "The ethnic factor serves the leaders more often than the leaders serve an ethnic entity" (Tishkov 1997, 71).

3. Ethnicity and world order

Studies of the emerging structure of international relations have reflected the identified differences in approaches to understanding ethnicity. Some scholars pointed to two fundamental tendencies in world development—globalization and regional integration on the one hand, and fragmentation and appearance of numerous mono-ethnic and weak states on the other (Rubinski 2002; Manykin 2001, 307-308). Consistent with the identified methodological division, those favoring the ideas of substantialism put emphasis on the ethnonationalist resistance to globalization processes, whereas relationists concentrate in their studies on the flexible adaptation of ethno-identities to globalization. While differing in their political beliefs, both groups acknowledge an exceptionally high potential for global conflicts that might result from the nexus of ethnicity and politics.

Those favoring the relationist position acknowledge the risks associated with the rise of ethnic consciousness, but also observe its possible relationship to the globalization processes. Thus, Rubinski (2002) draws attention to the coexistence and even mutual strengthening of the two described tendencies— economic, scientific, technological, and social unification versus growing aspirations to preserve national and civilizational identity of peoples. In Rubinski's view:

> The solution to this contradiction, which lies behind most of the internal and international conflicts after the Cold War, can only be found in acknowledging the validity of identity, inter-dependence, and solidarity of all world centers in the context of common risks and opportunities in the third millennium (2002, 161).

Other researchers are much more pessimistic. They perceive the two identified tendencies as an unsolvable conflict between the desired (globalization) and the actual (ethnification). According to Maksimenko (1999, 88):

we are not witnessing "globalization" but rather something opposite to it—regionalization and fragmentation of social relations, exacerbated by demographic pressures, as well as *ethnification of consciousness* that is vigorously developing in response to the destructive impact of globalization strategies.

Utkin (2002) speaks from a position close to substantialism in his characterization of contemporary international relations as the rise of traditionalism and ethno-nationalism. Arguing along the lines of Huntington (1996), Utkin describes "the marking point of the century's end as the transformation of human conflicts into ones with totally destructive outcomes due to the involvement of essentially traditionalist and religious ethnicities" (2002, 415, 418, 421). He finds the rise of traditionalism in peoples' return to their primordial values on all continents—in the Middle East, Africa, parts of South Asia and Latin America (2001, 171). The world, once divided into the first, second, and third, has now become split into six civilizational complexes.

Il'yin suggests something different. He also sees the world's ethnic diversity as a barrier to globalization. In his view, "despite all of the world's 'objective' unity, its fragmentation—from ecological and ethnic to civilizational and social class—persists and sometimes even heightens due to the opening to the global context" (2001, 188). The structures of the diagnosed "fragmented orders"—ethnic groups, clans, civilizations, corporations, nations, classes, etc.—do not disappear or lose their influence when faced with the structures of "global order." Yet they do not necessarily conflict with each other; in reality the "new morphological characteristics do not suppress or replace the old ones, but rather supplement them—effectively, although not always noticeably" (Il'yin 2001, 188).

Finally, Panarin's conceptual development (2002) stands out among the scholars of interrelation between globalization and ethno-national factors. With no visible connections to either substantialist or relationist approaches, Panarin's critique is aimed at what he sees as USA's "dehumanizing" project, its utmost disregard for national values of the world's majority, and self-serving manipulation of these values. He views the globalist American project as an "ethnocentric one that continues and at the same time distorts the ideas of

Enlightenment, with its characteristic emphasis on a single-dimensional actor and the ambition to master the world" (Panarin 2002, 219). This child of Enlightenment "cannot be confined to any ethnic or tribal values ...Its ethnic, racial, class, and other characteristics are nothing in comparison to its universal and rational nature." However, modern Western liberalism has betrayed the Enlightenment principle of universal social space and the Enlightenment's regard for people's ethnic and confessional differences. Against the spirit of Enlightenment, globalization is ethnocentric, not universal. It has been imposed on humanity despite its desire to preserve the institution of national sovereignty, at the price of ethnic separatism. The result, in Panarin's view, is that individual autonomy gets dissolved and becomes replaced by autonomy of the tribe. "Globalism paradoxically becomes tribalism" (Panarin 2002, 257).

4. Understanding ethnic identity

The above-identified methodological differences are also visible in Russian identity research. The question of how independent the effects of ethnicity are remains a highly contested issue between primordialists and instrumentalists. The core question is whether ethnic groups are considered direct actors or participants in foreign policy and international relations. That is to say, is ethnic entity the main politically significant substance, or is it one of many other substances and therefore a factor of relative significance? It is exactly at this point that scholars' opinions diverge principally, reinforcing their methodological differences.

Representatives of the substantialist approach attribute to ethnicity a status of central significance by placing it in the middle of their political universe. They assume ethnic identity to be given rather than something that needs to be problematized or researched empirically. The instrumentalists or relationists, however, insist that the "identity" concept is the central subject for investigation. Many Russian scholars are convinced that the central issue of modernity is whether existing civilizations can manage to preserve their identities or if these identities will be dissolved in some universal western-centric world. According to Rashkovski and Khoros, rethinking of civilizational identity and national cultural heritage in some cases, for example, in Latin America or in Russia, becomes a fundamental precondition for "overcoming serious crisis tendencies inflicted upon these societies" (Vostok-Zapad-Rossiya, 257). Unlike substantialists, relationists treat group identities as ontologically pluralistic and grounded in individual conscience. Malakhov notes that:

> Since the mid-1980s, political scientists have been discussing international relations actors as if these have competing "identities" ("Islamic," "Christian," "Western," "Eastern," "Eurasian," etc.). In reality, however, such entities are not resilient and are split into numerous smaller ones. Ultimately, each of these groups is made of individuals, who choose to identify themselves as members of one group or another (2001, 78).

In his other work (1998), Malakhov develops the concept of identity as primarily individually established rather than determined by external environment. He also identifies process and situation-related features of ethnicity and further suggests that although the impact of "material" characteristics on identity is decisive, it is ultimately the process of social communication that creates a system of meanings.

Russian social scientists have learned to appreciate the analytical difficulties of understanding the nature of identity. First of these difficulties is that identities come and express themselves on multiple levels, such as the micro-level (individuals), the macro-level (national state), as well as mega-levels (civilizational complexes and religious confessions). Second, studying identity requires familiarity with a plurality of research methods and approaches, including psychological and psychoanalytical, sociological, historic-cultural, historical-philosophical, politological, geopolitical, and others. Many researchers of these multiple identity levels and characters existing in modern society often pose their main question as follows: If the identified multiplicity of features is inherent to individual identity, is it also typical of other levels of identity formation (e.g., a level of territorial and political entity)?

For instance, the American social scientist Laitin (1998) develops the notion of "conglomerate identity" in his analysis of ethnic diasporas:

> Conglomerate identity is a membership category, a common denominator for the majority of identified groups that develop

some features different from the dominant traits of their society... Conglomerate identities are often formed when the
members of the dominant society perceive differing groups in
a similar way..., but groups with conglomerate identity can
also emerge when social borders dividing all related groups
residing on a foreign territory (as in the case of Ukrainians
and Russians living nowadays in Kazakhstan) are relatively
weak (Laitin 1998, 31).

Building on this notion, some Russian researchers (Bogaturov and Vinogradov 2000) drew attention to the "identity—modernization processes" nexus
and identified some long-lasting and relatively steady coexisting ties among
different social groups that can be referred to as conglomerate societies.
Cross-ties among Russian, Chechen, and Ingush ethnicities, or Jewish-Arab-
Palestinian, or Russian-Estonian, or Russian-Latvian ethnicities might be
responsible for the emergence of various conglomerate types. However, traditional or ethnic enclaves, according to these scholars, continue to perform
some vital regulatory functions even as modernization processes develop. The
vitality of such traditional ties is especially visible in the persistence of tribal
and clan relationships in the Caucasus, South-East Europe, and Muslim
republics inside Russia (Bogaturov and Vinogradov 2000, 112, 115, 116). A
conglomerate then is viewed as a form of self-organization and adaptation to
the conditions of modern and post-modern society, rather than as something
that impedes such adaptation.

The relationship between geopolitical and civilizational identities is yet
another question that occupies researchers. The former is often viewed as the
state's geographical attribute that defines the internal/external boundaries.
The latter, however, is a larger cultural affiliation that incorporates individual,
ethnic, or state attributes. The two identities interact and interweave, and
researchers identify the so-called inter-civilizational peoples that reside
between larger cultural entities (civilizations), or on civilizational periphery
(e.g., East Europeans, Caucasians, Turks, Mongolians and others, residing in
East Asia on the border of China and Russia). These people do not belong to
the core communities of neighboring civilizations (Islamic, Chinese, Indian,
Japanese, Russian, or North Atlantic). They have to establish themselves cul-

turally, politically and economically with regard to these communities. Because of their "peripheral" location, they either feel discriminated against or find their status suitable for some "strategic self-adjustment" (Tsymburski 2001, 78).

Finally, it is important to point out that the rise of interest to identity *problematique* is connected to the development of feminist research in the humanities and social sciences. Feminists have drawn our attention to the multiplicity of identity through their critique of mainstream paradigms in the theory of international relations—Realism, Pluralism, and Structuralism/Globalizm—for ignoring the very issue of cultural meanings and for their narrow methodological and positivist orientation (Zalevski and Enlo 2002, 309). The identity problem in contemporary international relations is extremely complicated and includes not only ethnic, racial, confessional, and linguistic dimensions, but also gender, socio-economic, and social-professional dimensions. Some social scientists apply the technique of factor analysis to better capture this complex identity incorporating ethno-national as well as territorial components. For example, Petrella (2002) identified the following factors in researching the multi-level structure of identity:

(1)   cultural identity or a set of characteristics viewed as national character;

(2)   specific language characteristics; above all, the standardized language that continues to fulfill some vital social function, and whose disappearance will likely have some serious negative consequences for individual and collective identity;

(3)   politico-constitutional status of a region, before and after its inclusion into a nation-state;

(4)   relative level of economic development and economic potential;

(5)   degree of economic self-sufficiency.

In Petrella's judgment:

> as obvious as it might seem, it is rather difficult to identify the presence or absence of a cultural identity or a set of national characteristics. The main issue is not what a nation is, but rather to what extent it is the subject of symbolic representa-

tion, significance and, identification that is perceived and accepted as such by region's inhabitants, as well as by outsiders (2002, 236).

From this analytical perspective, Scotland, Wales, the Basque Country, Catalonia, and Flanders can be considered as the holders of territorial national identities in Western Europe. Petrella views Wallonia and the Canary Islands of the early 1980s in the stage of their identity formation. One could also speak of territorial identity of active minorities in Galicia, Brittany, Corsica, and Sardinia. In the past, Scotland, Wales, Catalonia, Brittany all had independent and sovereign status. Relative economic autonomy was characteristic of some parts (but not of ethnic regions in general) of the Basque Country, Flanders, Wallonia, Friesland, and others.[1]

5. Ethnic conflicts

Finally, Russian IR scholars have developed both a theoretical and a practical interest in studying ethnic conflicts. This is a broad set of issues wghich includes conflicts of national and regional scope that continue to spread as a result of the collapse of the bipolar international system. It also includes the issue of defending minority rights—ethnic, racial, religious, linguistic, and cultural. Furthermore, it involves the issue of threat posed by extremism and terrorism so long as these phenomena are tied to ethnicity. Last but not least, ethno-political autonomy, separatism, secessionism, irredentism, and so on, can be also added to the list of issues related to ethnic conflicts. In the Russian context, the discipline that studies this range of issues is referred to as ethno-political conflict resolution. In their analyses of the origins of ethnic conflicts, researchers often establish a link to the end of Westphalia system's monopoly on state power and to the prevalence of state forms of identity. An authoritative reference book states:

> the new world situation (which can be considered as transitional, including on the level of human consciousness) cre-

---

[1] Vladislav Kaganski (1995) develops a different factor analysis to examine post-Soviet regionalization.

ates various identity problems, such as the appearance of multiple or mixed forms of self-identification. The resulting phenomena—attempts at ethnic and religious self-identification—often lead to conflicts (Kategorii 2002, 623).

Specialists note that ethno-political tensions have emerged as the defining attribute of contemporary world order (Lebedeva 2003, 190). Such tensions are typical of approximately 160 zones on the planet (Neklessa 2001, 63). Despite the complexity of the phenomenon under study, Russian scholars have made certain progress in the theoretical conceptualization of ethno-political conflicts. The works of Lebedeva, Pain, and Popov have played a particularly important role in this respect.[2] Below I briefly characterize some of their most important theoretical contributions. One key disagreement in the literature concerns the role of structural versus procedural factors in ethnic conflicts' emergence and resolution. Lebedeva and Pain acknowledge the significance of both factors, whereas Popov puts a special emphasis on the role of procedural factors.

Lebedeva (2000) offers an analysis of two ontological layers in an attempt to find peaceful resolutions of conflicts: 1) structural factors or series of independent variables (structure of society, level of economic development, and others); and 2) procedural factors or dependent variables (politics pursued by the participants of a conflict, as well as by the third party). While analyzing conflicts in Northern Ireland, Belgium, the former Yugoslavia, the former Czechoslovakia, Chechnya, and Tatarstan, Lebedeva identifies the following structural factors: existence of different ethnic groups and/or confessions with relatively clear administrative divisions and national territories, significant regional differentiation, substantial social and political changes and the appearance of new elites, undeveloped institutions and mechanisms of conflict resolution, and underdevelopment of a culture of public consensus. The more of such factors

---

[2]   The Russian literature on ethnic conflicts is rather large. See especially the volume by Arutunyan, Drobizheva, and Susokolov (1998, 229-260), for a detailed overview. Most publications are devoted to analysis of causes, dynamics, and prospects of conflict resolution in the post-Soviet space, mostly in Russia and the near abroad, as well as in the former Yugoslavia. One can also find comparative research, for example on the Kosovo and Chechen conflicts (Miroporyadok posle Balkanskogo krizisa 2000, 162-221).

exist, the more serious is the conflict situation. In considering procedural factors, the author proposes to take the differentiation between unilateral and collaborative action as a point of departure. Thus, the unilateral approach did not become dominant in peacefully resolved conflicts (Belgium, former Czechoslovakia, Tatarstan). Where unilateralism gained the upper hand, however, military actions prevailed over peaceful solutions (Yugoslavia and Chechnya).

Lebedeva's understanding of conflict dynamics is related to her methodology. During the first phase of the conflict, its threshold and potential are defined by structural dynamics. The second, culmination phase, gives a special role to mostly procedural factors. The third phase comes after culmination, when the conflict is resolved. The whole methodological framework leads to the following conclusion: structural factors formulate the conflict situation, and procedural ones define the form of its resolution (Lebedeva, 38). Works of Pain are comparable with Lebedeva's structurally procedural approach. According to Pain (2002), three factors contribute to the growth of extremism and terrorism—unfinished modernization, inadequate state policies, and ideologists, or organizers of extremist actions. Therefore, three symmetrical processes—societal modernization, establishment of new state policies, and support for anti-extremism ideology—must counter-balance the above-mentioned factors.[3]

Supporters of the predominantly processual perspective take a different approach to the problem. Tishkov, in his definition of ethnic conflict, leaves no role for the factors of structural order: "Ethnic conflict implies any form of civil resistance on internal and international levels, when at least one of the parties is organized upon the ethnic principle or acts in the name of an ethnic group" (Tishkov 1997, 309). Developing this approach, Prazauskas (1997) suggests that structural incompatibility of the ethnic groups' interests is "atypical and rare. As a rule, a relatively small portion of an ethnic group may get directly involved in interethnic dispute, and in the best case scenario, it may enjoy only passive support from the majority" (Prazauskas 1999, 220-221). Both authors

---

[3] Based upon analysis of conflict resolution in the zones of ethnic instability (Chechnya, Somali, and Afghanistan), Pain (2002) formulates a range of practical ideas for maintaining control over situations of ethnic tension.

pay special attention to the symbolic, often irrational, dimensions of a conflict. In their view, social and psychological complexes, exacerbated feelings of danger, exaltation, symbolic perceptions of territory and national language (Tishkov), as well as collective historical memory (Prazauskas) are the factors that make ethnic conflicts more pervasive and dangerous than those of social and class nature. On that basis, both scholars argue against the emergence of some general theory of ethnic and interethnic conflicts in the near future (Tishkov 1997; Prazauskas 1997).

Popov (1997) also emphasizes the factors of processual and instrumental order, pointing especially to the role played by ethnic and religious elites in mobilizing and consolidating groups involved in a conflict. He identifies three stages in the process of such mobilization. The first stage involves what he refers to as "emotional actualization of xenophobia" or a series of ways to aggravate some mental traumas of an ethnic consciousness. The second stage is that of "groups' political orientation," at which they actively bring in political programs aiming to achieve further mobilization of an ethnic group. Finally, the third stage involves "moral legitimations of violence," which justifies a potential bloodshed on behalf of a nation or ethnic group's highest interests.

In conclusion, one should say that despite its relative youthfulness, Russian studies of ethnicity have emerged as a growing and vibrant research program that is already marked by some accomplishments. Russian scholars do not yet fully realize the connection existing between theoretical disputes on ethnicity and the new world order on the one hand, and empirical research of conflicts and identities on the other. Yet, such a connection does exist, and it needs to be fully articulated in order to provide a new impulse for development of ethnonational studies in Russian international relations. Furthermore, new research in the area is in a process of developing dialogue and interaction with Western researchers. Results of such interaction can be rather fruitful.

References

Arutyunyan, Yy. V., L. M. Drobizheva, A .A. Susokolov. 1998. Etnosotsiologia. Aspekt-Press, Moskva.

Belkov, O. A. 2001. Teoreticheskiye osnovy vneshnepoliticheskoi deyatelnosti Rossii. RAGS, Moskva.

Bogaturov, A. D. and A. V. Vinogradov. 2000. Anklavno-konglomerativny tip razvitiya. Vostok-Zapad-Rossiya.

Boroday, Yu. 1995. Puti stanovleniya natsional'nogo edinstva. Nash sovremennik 1.

Guseynov, G., D. Dragunski, S. Sergeyev, V. Tsymburski. 1990. Etnos i politicheskaya vlast'. Vek XX i mir 4.

Huntington, S. 1996. Clash of Civilizations and the Remaking of World Order. Simon & Shuster, New York.

Il'ukhin, V. I. 1999. Natsiya-gosudarstvo-bezopasnost'. Tsentrkniga, Moskva.

Il'yin, M. V. 2001. Stabilizatsiya razvitiya. In: Megatrendy mirovogo razvitiya. Ekonomika, Moskva.

Kagansky, V. 1995. Sovetskoe prostranstvo: konstruktsiya i dekonstruktsiya. In: Inoe. Khrestomatiya novogo rossiyskogo samosoznaniya. No publisher information, Moskva.

Kategorii politicheskoi nauki. 2002. No publisher information, Moskva.

Latin, D. 1998. Identity in Formation. Cornell University Press, Ithaca.

Lebedeva, M. M. 2000. Mezhetnicheskie konflikty na rubezhe vekov. Mirovaya ekonomika i mezhdunarodnye otnosheniya 5.

Lebedeva, M. M. 2003. Mirovaya politika. Aspekt Press, Moskva.

Malakhov, V. S. 1998. Neudobstva s identichnostyu. Voprosy filosofii 2.

Malakhov, V. S. 2001. Identichnost'. In: Novaya filosofskaya entsiklopediya. No publisher information, Moskva.

Manykin, A. 2001. Vvedeniye v teoriyu mezhdunarodnykh otnosheniyi. MGU, Moskva.

Maksimenko, V. 1999. Proiskhodit li "globalizatsiya"? Pro et Contra 4 (4).

Miroporyadok posle Balkanskogo krizisa: novye realnosti menyayushchegosya mira. 2000. Dobrosvet, Moskva.

Neklessa, A. 2000. Konets epokhi Bol'shogo Moderna. In: Miroporyadok posle Balkanskogo krizisa: novye realnosti menyayushchegosya mira. Dobrosvet, Moskva.

Pain, E. 2002. O prirode etnicheskogo i religioznogo ekstremizma. Vestnik Instituta Kennana v Rossii 1.

Panarin, A. S. 2002. Iskusheniye globalizmom. EKSMO-Press, Moskva.

Petrella, R. 2002. Natsionalisticheskiye i regionalnye dvizheniya v Zapadnoi Yevrope. In: Etnos i politika. No publisher information, Moskva.

Pivovarov, Yu. S. 2002. Istoriografiya ili antropologiya? In: Globalizatsiya: Konflikt ili dialog tsivilizatsiyi? INION, Moskva.

Platonov, Yu. P. 2002. Etnicheski faktor: geopolitika i psikhologiya. Rech', Sankt-Peterburg.

Popov, A. 1997. Prichiny vozniknoveniya i dinamika razvitiya konfliktov. In: Identichnost' i konflikt v postsovetskikh gosudarstvakh. Carnegie Center, Moskva.

Prazauskas, A. 1997. The Ingridients of State Unity. Pro et Contra 2 (2).

Rubinski, Yu. I. 2002. Yevropeyskaya tsivilizatsiya v menyayushchemsya mire. In: Globalizatsiya. Konflikt ili dialog tsivilizatsi? INION, Moskva.

Tishkov, V. A. 1997. Ocherki teorii i politiki etnichnosti v Rossii. Institut etnologii i antropologii RAN, Moskva.

Tsymburski, V. L. 2001. Identichnost' tsivilizatsionnaya. In: Novaya filosofskaya entsiklopedia. No publisher information, Moskva.

Utkin, A. I. 2002. Vyzov Zapada i otvet Rossii. Algoritm, Moskva.

Utkin, A. I. 2001. Globalizatsiya: protsess i osmysl'eniye. Logos, Moskva.

Verderi, K. Kuda idut "natsiya" i "natsionalizm"? In: Natsii i natsionalizm. No publisher information, Moskva.

Zalevski, M. and S. Enlo. 2002. Voprosy identichnosti v mezhdunarodnykh otnosheniyakh. In: Teoriya mezhdunarodnykh otnosheniyi na rubezhe stoletii. No publisher information, Moskva.

VIII. The study of international political economy in Russia

Stanislav L. Tkachenko

The purpose of this article is to examine the development of International Political Economy in contemporary Russia—its academic study and research application in the theory of international relations.

I. International political economy: Western and Russian roots

International political economy (IPE) is a subdiscipline of international relations (IR) that analyzes interactions between private economic actors and states.[1] Relatively new in the Western academia, IPE is only in its formative stages in Russia, with its own peculiarities and characteristics. An interest in this discipline in Russia is related to the emancipation from isolationist Marxist-Leninist dogmas, as well as the appearance in the Russian context of some pressing new issues that the Western political economy had been studying all along. The issues are the following: What is the advantage of free trade over mercantilism and autarky? Is market economy the most important precondition for a nation's rapid economic growth? What is the connection between market economy and the nations' desire to live in peace with their neighbors? Why have some countries been among the leaders in industrial development over centuries, while others have lagged behind even while possessing abundant natural resources? The fact that these questions are becoming critical for Russian political scientists creates favorable conditions to focus the nation's attention on developing IPE within Russian IR.

---

[1] There is no consensus among the scholars of Europe and North America regarding the definition of the term "International Political Economy". This can be explained, to a significant degree, by the fact that every definition is never fully free from its author's values and ideas. For an overview, see Gilpin 1987.

Western IPE

International Political Economy became an established part of International Relations when Western realities called for a better understanding of new patterns in the development of world economy and their relationship to the political context. In the 1960-1970s, many of the North American and West European political scientists and economists came to realize that the separate developments of their disciplines had their limitations when it came to extending our overall knowledge about world political and economic processes. IPE was able to go beyond the limitations of traditional IR theories by modifying the two established approaches—Realism (concepts of power, might, conflict) and Liberalism (justice, international law, cooperation). Based upon the availability of new data, scholars demonstrated their ability to analyze some new phenomena in interstate affairs, such as European economic and political integration. In so doing, they built on some already existing theories, such as neofunctionalism, and produced plethora of new ones.

IPE scholars went beyond the limits of economics and focused their attention on the analysis of political connections to the state and the role of the state in the world economy. On the other hand, political economy expanded its interest to history and historical dynamics, which moved the newly emerged discipline further away from the neoclassical economic tradition. This process was well summarized by Whallen (1996, 3), who noted that political economy took into account the factor of time by placing political events into historical context of interactions between individuals and social institutions. Political economy therefore fully recognizes that individuals, institutions, as well as knowledge and values, are historical products and are subject to change.

Russian roots

Due to principally different conditions, IPE in Russia is developing in a different way. One can identify two of these Russia-specific conditions.

First, the Marxist isolation of the country and its science from the rest of the world has led to a hypertrophy of state power and to the extension of state involvement in the life of society. Granted, there were many arguments and disagreements within the Soviet Marxist approach that can be traced to the clashes between Bukharin and Stalin regarding the pace of the country's industrialization and collectivization. There were also disagreements in the Soviet post-war political economy, such as the one between Evgeni Varga on the one hand, and Zhdanov and Stalin on the other. While Varga thought that capitalism in Europe and the USA had relatively stabilized, his opponents continued to emphasize the depth of imperialistic contradictions and the inevitability of capitalist decline. These differences continued to matter after Stalin's death, with Stalinists gathering around the editor-in-chief of *Kommunist* and member of the Central Committee of the Communist Party Richard Kosolapov, and with Marxists of quasi social-democratic orientation centering at the Institute of World Economics and International Relations that had been originally headed by Varga. It should be noted, however, that both schools worked within the same Marxist paradigm which allowed only limited freedom of thought and prohibited any kind of creative thinking regarding the role of the Soviet state.[2]

The truth is that within the Marxist paradigm, IPE could only be one-sided and poorly developed. One needs only to recall how the Soviet scientists voluntarily applied Marxism in their work. Such a tendency significantly narrowed the opportunities for researchers, especially those studying the complex interconnections between the world economic and political processes. It is hardly accidental that while some disciplines, such as geopolitics, have been flourishing in the post-Soviet Russia, there are still very few national publications in the area of IPE.

Secondly, the Marxist isolation implied the priority of security issues: the Soviet leaders viewed opportunities presented by the world economy exclusively as threats to the whole existence of the USSR from the hostile capitalist surrounding. The degree of proper attention to the politico-economic affairs in the world was low, and social scientists routinely perceived the world as a zero sum game between the "world of capitalism" and the "world of socialism."

---

2   In Pavel A. Tsygankov's characterization of IR development in the USSR, all theories progressed "within the same methodological paradigm and had to be linked to Marxism" (Tsygankov 2000, 7).

2. The Soviet break-up and the painful birth of post-Soviet IPE

The new context

Following the disintegration of the USSR, the social context of the development of political science in Russia had changed in a major way. Adaptation to
the realities of the world economy has come to replace Marxist isolationist
practices. The transition to a capitalist market economy has come to substitute
the methods of the administrative-socialist regulation. Russia has found itself
in a new international surrounding and now has to adapt to new conditions of
economic cooperation with its nearest neighbors—the Newly Independent
States—and the rest of the world.

It is important to acknowledge that Russia holds an unimpressive place in
the world economy. With the United States' GDP accounting for 21% of the
world level, the European Union about 21%, Japan 8%, China 7%, the 1.7%
contribution of the Russian Federation looks fairly insignificant. According to
some of the most favorable estimates, Russia might be able to increase its
share by the year of 2015 to only 2% (Tkachenko 2000a, 54). Besides its slow
progress, Russia continues to be largely isolated from the world economy, and
this is while regional economic integration has emerged as one of the key dis-
tinctive feature of global development. Japan, South Korea, China, ASEAN,
and other nations are getting ready to act on their vision of East Asian economic integration outlined on November 1999. The EU also occupies a prominent place among regions of the globe.

Russian researchers then face a host of new problems: Which rules and
principles must be followed in developing economic relations within the CIS
(Commonwealth of Independent States) and with the states of the former
USSR? Should Russia join the WTO, and if so, under which conditions? How
should Russia build the relationship with the EU, the largest regional association west of Russia? At which pace should Russia try to expand its economic
presence in the Asian-Pacific region? How should it stimulate its internal economic development? Whom should Russia count upon in attracting foreign
economic aid and investments? (Smirnov 2001)

Schools and debates

There are several politico-economic schools of thought in Russia that attempt to provide answers to the above questions. Dynkin (2002) distinguishes two schools that address the question of global economic integration strategy: liberal institutionalists and dirigists. One can also identify the world system school. The resulting triple classification is close to the division into Liberals, Realists, and Marxists typical of the Western IPE (Gilpin 1987, chap. 1).

Liberal Institutionalists put emphasis on the development of an institutional environment, continuation of reforms, reduction of share of non-market sectors in the economy, support of small and medium-size business, and on balancing the budget and increasing its effectiveness (Dynkin 2002). Liberal economic theories often propose similar guidelines for nations in the process of transition from communism. This group promotes Russia's aggressive integration into the world economy, membership in the WTO, and expansion of relations with the EU, arguing that such integration steps would favor the creation of an institutional environment conducive to economic development. Market-institutional principles must also be applied to the development of relationships within the former USSR (Tkachenko 2003).

Dirigists insist upon the necessity of introducing a special tax levied upon export sectors and a centralized redistribution of resources in favor of the processing industry. The ideal for this group is a mobilized economy with a significant role of the state. The logic of dirigism is close to that of the Realist approach in Western IPE, and it is adopted by those who link Russia's survival and prosperity to the state's ability to regulate foreign investment flows and the creation of Russian private companies. It is assumed that such companies would invest overseas, thereby helping the state to realize its foreign policy goals (Movsisyan and Ognivtsev 1999; Kochetov 1994).

Dirigists are also close in their views to the ideas of the neo-Marxist theory of modern world system, which offers similar strategies for moving the periphery countries closer to the center of the world economic development. Thus Alexandr Neklessa, one of the authors of the fundamental study "The Post-Industrial World and Russia" (Khoros and Krasilshikov 2001) shares one of the main arguments of Emmanuel Wallerstein's world system theory,[3] which implies the following: Russia belongs to the deep South and is on "the outskirts of civilization," where "social actors do not survive the pressure of the new global pyramid." Fursov (1996) also comes close to this position. He sees Russia as a "counterweight" to the Western economic model, which is reminiscent of the "semi-periphery" or even "periphery" in Wallerstein's theory. It is important to emphasize, however, that in the West, those sharing such views associate themselves with Neo-Marxism, while Russian scholars pay considerably less attention to traditional Marxist economic analysis. Rather, their views are closer to the discipline of geopolitics.

Both dirigists and supporters of the world system theory are critical of the ideas of Liberal Institutionalists in regard to Russia's economic development and integration to the world economy. Both schools consider economic self-reliance, political autonomy, and priority relationships with the countries of the former USSR as extremely important. Among dirigists, economists are often the ones who set the agenda. Using economic theories and statistical data, Russian economists try to argue that international economic institutions are incapable of solving the problem of a growing gap between the North and the South (that is to say, between rich and poor states). This group is fearful of Russia opening up its markets to international competition. The key influence on the group comes from the nationally oriented business sectors, united under the Russian Chamber of Commerce, headed by the former prime-minister, Yevgeni Primakov. In principle, dirigists do not speak against joining the WTO, but they do insist that any rush to membership in the organization is dangerous for the Russian economy and that the whole process requires time and preparation.[4]

---

[3] A recently published book of Wallerstein (2001) has been important in terms of presenting this view to the Russian reader.

[4] There is no devastating critique of the WTO in Russian scholarly literature, and every serious researcher admits that, in general, joining the WTO is a positive step (e.g., Liventsev and Lisovolik 2002, 3, 340-341).

3. The future of Russian IPE: problems and possible solutions

Problem I: The separation of political science and economics

International economics was an established discipline during the Soviet period. The discipline studied and continues to study economic relations between individual states that involve trade and investments, as well as the interactions between non-state actors (transnational corporations) and the integrated economy in the field of industrial production and services. The educational and teaching level of international economics in Russian Academy of Sciences' institutions has been fairly high since the times of the Soviet Union. But the main credit must be given to "pure" economists, those who rarely refer in their works to historical facts and methods of historical analysis, outside of economic theories and statistical data.

After the dissolution of the USSR and the elimination of ideological limitations in the study of international relations, many Russian IR researches focused their attention on issues of international security. Geopolitics became the most popular approach to analyze an international problem. Within the first post-Soviet decade, very few Russian researchers were able to go beyond the limits of those approaches and themes. There were practically no publications in the field of IPE in Russia. Russian scholars of the 1990s repeated the error of a continuous separation of economics from political science, which their Western colleagues had managed to overcome back in the 1960s-1970s. There was a big difference between the content and methods of political scientists and economists in the field of international relations. The former concentrated their efforts on interstate political relations, as well as on the political side of interstate economic interactions. In their turn, the latter rarely paid any serious attention to the distinction between domestic and international economic relations in their research. Economists applied their traditional methods of mathematical analysis and did not include any ideas from political economy. In my view, this inter-disciplinary gap has not been bridged as yet, and Russian specialists in international relations have not even become fully aware of its existence.

Annual congresses of RISA—the Russian International Studies Association—can help to illustrate the above mentioned tendency. The last congress, which took place in Moscow in June 2002, had only one panel session devoted to IPE issues. The session was titled "New approaches in the study of international political economy" and included presentations by scholars from Finland (Heikki Patomaki), Sweden (Anna Leander), and Romania (Paul Dragos Aligica). The Romanian scholar was the head of the panel, and Bastiaan van Apeldoorn from Amsterdam Vrije Universiteit was the commentator. Symptomatically, no Russian scholar took part in the panel, and the very rationale for including the topic of IPE into the congress's agenda had to do with research of foreign participants working in this field of IR. The lack of interest to IPE in Russia is even more noticeable when compared to the popularity of IPE in the United States and Western Europe. For instance, in the predominantly American International Studies Association (ISA), the IPE section is one of the largest, and it regularly boasts the largest number of plenary sessions at its annual conventions.

There is a strong and growing interest to the integrated study of politics and economy in Europe. For example, at the XVI Annual Congress of the European Economic Association, which took place in August-September of 2001 in Lausanne, there was a section titled "Political Economy." Among its main topics were the impact of constitutions of developed democratic European nations on the process of governance and stability within Europe at large (Diermeier, Eraslan, and Merlo 2002), as well the impact of constitutionally defined electoral procedures on the size of governments and effectiveness of their activity (Persson and Tabellini 2002). Presently, it is hard to imagine similar research conducted by Russian scholars of international relations. These topics, however, could be critically important for developing a better understanding of Russia's executive power potential to carry out its responsibilities effectively.

Fortunately, the situation is far from hopeless and has began to change for the better. Scholars have started to pay more attention to IPE developments. Thus the international relations textbook by Pavel A. Tsygankov included a chapter devoted to IPE—an important symbol for spreading knowledge of IPE in Russia. Given the small number of IR textbooks in Russia, such a chapter is likely to further stimulate interest in the discipline of IPE among both students and scholars. However, one word of criticism is warranted. Tsygankov wrote about IPE in the context of Marxist developments and titled his chapter "International political economy and Neo-Marxism" (2002, 140-55). Perhaps such an analytical angle is justified, taking into consideration the long dominance of the Marxist-Leninist tradition in the USSR. Still, one should have noted that neo-Marxist approaches in IPE can hardly be called the most influential in the field of international relations. Although the Marxist tradition developed the important world system approach, tracing the origins and—even more—the main achievements of IPE to Marxism does not do full justice to the field.[5]

One can only hope that the identified gap in research of Russian economists and political scientists will be reduced in the near future. This would be essential in order to improve our understanding of many complicated processes in the international arena and would have both political and economic significance for Russia and other nations in the world.

Problem II: A deficit of theoretical generalizations

Works of Russian researches that analyze the issues of world economy and foreign economic policy lack theoretical generalizations. As a rule, authors limit themselves to committing to one of the two "extremes"—liberalism, associated with monetarism in theory and Margaret Thatcher-like policies in practice, and what can be conditionally defined as "state-centrism" or "state-oriented" approach (Il'yin and Inozemtsev 2001, 81; Bychkova 2001, 163). The latter, however, might include a wide range of recommendations about strengthening the role of the state in economic affairs, from those similar to recommendations of John M. Keynes to those of mobilizing the economy in the manner of Stalin's socialist management.[6] In general, the neo-liberal approach is compatible with the IPE's definition of "liberalism," but the "state-

---

[5]   In his other work, Tsygankov returns to the role of IPE in the development of IR theory and draws upon the works of Susan Strange, who viewed the central issue of IPE differently from Marxists—as that of relations between the state and the markets (Tsygankov 2002, 34).

[6]   See the author's monograph in which he examines the range and applicability of the ideas of IPE with regard to the world's economic history in the early 20th century (Tkachenko 2000b, 16-22, 182).

centrism" often combines the ideas of both the nationalist school (such as the theory of hegemonic stability) and those of Marxism (such as the world system theory).

The lack of theoretical generalizations in the works of Russian scholars is typical even of publications in serious academic journals. Symptomatically, in his review of a collective volume on globalization,[7] one author writes that "the book can benefit from a more diverse empirical coverage and a more solid theoretical systematization of empirical trends" (Kustarev 2002, 179). But it is practically impossible to provide such systematization without using the instruments of IPE.

In a rare article about political economy, published in the journal *Politicheskie issledovaniya*, the author (Bychkova 2002) discusses the application of concepts of IPE, but again refers to the work by economists, particularly of liberal orientation (Jeffrey Sachs, Anders Aslund, and Joseph Stiglitz). Although the author makes an effort to explore some political science concepts, the resulting synthesis is rather mechanical—the ideas from economics co-exist with those from political science, but are not really integrated into a coherent theory. Part of the problem is that the author, as many others, does not take seriously Russia's very peculiar experience, which might have challenged the preconceived notions and pushed theory in a more creative direction. Overall, this article in a leading Russian journal has practically disregarded IPE issues.

Problem III: the weakness of educational curriculum

Finally, the weakness of the academic and educational foundation accounts for another problem in the development of Russian IPE. While it is possible to trace some ideas borrowed from Western IPE in Russian scholarly literature, there is practically no such effort in the field of teaching IPE.

As an exception, the author of the current essay might refer to his course for M.A. students of international relations at St. Petersburg State University. This course was developed in 1996 and could have not been possible without

---

[7] The book is Il'yin and Inozemtsev 2001.

invaluable assistance of Jonathan Aronson, John Odell and Steven Lamy of the University of Southern California.[8] The course is titled "Political aspects of international economic relations." Besides this course, one can speak of only one similar course taught in the tradition of "world economy" at Moscow State Institute of International Relations. Such a situation is totally unacceptable for Russia. Despite the presence of numerous textbooks on world economy that can be partially used in the academic process of teaching IPE, there is an acute need for a series of textbooks devoted to the subject of IPE. Since the subject requires a good knowledge of international relations theory, such a course should be taught either at the upper division undergraduate level or—which, in the author's view, is more preferable—during the first year of M.A. studies of the same concentration. Russian scholars should be expected to produce such textbooks in the near future.

Possible solutions

The situation with the development of IPE in Russia is serious but not hopeless. Its improvement is conditioned by three circumstances: 1) growing integration of Russia into the world economy; 2) active learning of Western conceptions and theories of IPE and 3) development of a general educational basis in the field of teaching this discipline.

Contemporary Russian realities are still studied primarily by economists and specialists in international relations. This should be considered a weakness of the Russian science of International Relations because it is impossible to fully understand the role of Russia in world politics without studying her links to the world economic processes. Most Russian researchers and theorists are still preoccupied with geopolitical issues, which often prevents them from realistically assessing their country's place in the world in terms of the already developed conceptual apparatus of global IPE. Eventually, however, a growing integration of Russia to the world economy should heighten an interest to the study of IPE as an academic discipline.

---

[8]   The syllabus is available at: http://www.dip.pu.ru/russian/education/program/prog15.htm

Probing and digesting the knowledge accumulated by the Western founders of this discipline over the three decades of its existence seems to be one of the most important priorities. One hopes that Western knowledge would be planted on a well prepared soil. The Marxist political economy legacy, while loosing its supporters in Russia, still has many supporters left in most of the academic institutions teaching international political and economic relations. The special interest of Russian researches to the issues of international security makes them somewhat predisposed to understand the logic and the experience of the hegemonic stability theory. This theory, of course, was developed to understand the role of the United States in the global economy, but it can be extended and applied to the integration processes in the post-Soviet space and to Russia's potential to serve as a hegemon responsible for initiating and maintaining such integration.[9]

In conclusion, one must note that, until Russian political scientists and economists stop being primarily interested in studying Russia's internal problems and begin taking seriously such issues as Russia's place on the international arena, its role in the international economic organizations, and its ability to effectively exploit the existing international regimes, IPE will continue to be a "stepchild" among other disciplines of international relations. An expansion of Russian scholarly research agenda in the direction of incorporating all these important issues can become an important precondition for the growth of interest to this discipline.

References

Bychkova, O. V. 2001. Post-sovetskiye rynochnyye reformy: Politiko-ekonomicheskiye kontseptsii. Polis 6.

Diermeier, D., H. Eraslan, A. Merlo. 2002. Coalition Governments and Comparative Constitutional Design. European Economic Review 46 (4-5).

---

[9] Sharing Tsygankov's concern that some core parts of this theory "are difficult to perceive and sometime they cause protest outside the West" (2002, 24), one might try to apply it to evaluate the current and future role of Russia in post-Soviet space, as well as Russia's economic potential in constructing a leadership position among the NIS (some of these problems are examined in Tkachenko and Petermann 2002).

Dynkin, A. 2002. Est' li u Rossii shans v global'noi ekonomike? Pro et Contra, 7, Spring.

Fursov, A.I. 1996. Kolokola istorii. INION, Moskva.

Gilpin, R. 1987. The Political Economy of International Relations. Princeton University Press, Princeton.

Il'yin, M. V. and V. L. Inozemtsev, eds. 2001. Megatrendy mirovogo razvitiya. Tsentr postindustrial'nykh issledovaniy, Moskva.

Khoros, V. and V. Krasil'schikov, eds. 2001. Post-Industrial'nyi mir i Rossiya. Editorial URSS, Moskva.

Kochetov, Ye. 1994. Geoekonomika i vneshneekonomicheskaya strategiya Rossii. Mirovaya ekonomika i mezhdunarodnyye otnosheniya 11.

Kustarev, A. 2002. Review of the collective monograph "Megatrendy mirovogo razvitiya." Pro et Contra 7, Spring.

Liventsev, N. N. and Y. D. Lisovolik. 2002. Aktual'nyye problemy prisoyedineniya Rossii k VTO. Ekonomika, Moskva.

Movsisyan, A. and S. Ognivtsev. 1999. Transnatsional'nyi kapital i natsional'nyye gosudarstva. Mirovaya ekonomika i mezhdunarodnyye otnosheniya 6.

Persson, T., G. Tabellini. 2002. Do Constitutions Cause Large Governments? Quasi-Experimental Evidence. European Economic Review 46 (4-5).

Smirnov, P. S. 2001. National'naya bezopasnost': voprosy torgovoi politiki. Ekonomicheskaya gazeta, Moskva.

Tkachenko, S. 2000a. Rashireniye ES i voprosy bezopasnosti Rossii. In: Rossiya i osnovnyye instituty bezopasnosti v Yevrope, ed. by D. Trenin. Carnegie Center, Moskva.

Tkachenko, S. L. 2000b. Currency Regulation at the Transition from the Gold Standard to the Fluctuating Rate of National Currency. St. Petersburg University, St. Petersburg.

Tkachenko, S. 2003. Russia's Membership in WTO: Implications for Economic Security of the Post-Soviet Countries. Paper presented at the Annual Convention of the International Studies Association, Portland, Oregon.

Tkachenko, S. and S. Petermann. 2002. Sotrudnichestvo stran SNG v voyennoi sfere i faktor NATO. St. Petersburg University, St. Petersburg.

Tsygankov, P. A. 2000. Teoriya mezhdunarodnykh otnosheniy. Gardarika, Moskva.

Tsygankov, P. A. 2002. Teoriya mezhdunarodnykh otnosheniy. Gardarika, Moskva.

Wallen, Ch. J., ed. 1996. Political Economy for the XXI Century: Contemporary Views on the Trend of Economics. M.E. Sharpe, New York.

Wallerstein, E. 2001. Analiz mirovykh sistem i situatsiyi v sovremennom mire. Universitskaya kniga, St. Petersburg.

IX. From prominence to decline: Russian studies of international negotiations

Marina M. Lebedeva

1. Introduction: negotiations and scholarship

Negotiations penetrate all spheres of human life and activity—politics, economy, and interpersonal relations. They are a very powerful instrument invented by humankind to resolve conflicts, settle disputes, and facilitate cooperation. It is not by chance that negotiations became an object of study of different disciplines—psychology, sociology, economics, law, international relations, and political science. Some scholars (Atkinson 1980) refer to negotiations as "the highest form of economic relations." Others (Held 1989) view them as a fundamental form of politics, which, along with conflict and cooperation, serve as a "bridge" in the transition from conflict to cooperation.

Originally, negotiations studies were the subject of political science and international relations, with their emphasis on conflict resolution. Some time later, however, the negotiation reality became complicated by application of multilateral, multilevel and multi-aspect approaches. As a result, researchers ceased to look at negotiations as a solution of political conflicts and moved toward some new areas, such as the European Union, ecological issues, and so on.

Negotiation studies reflect not only progress of social science, but also human and societal progress in general. In politics, for example, negotiations penetrate all aspects of democratic nations, but they are either non-existent or replaced by imitated quasi-negotiations in totalitarian societies.

Negotiation studies can be used to judge Russia's political development and the scholarly progress in international relations and political science. The Soviet era knew no research on political negotiations since political research in general was non-existent. The key ideological assumption was that all contradictions were to be resolved through class struggle in the process of socialist construction. Conflict was viewed as a zero-sum game that could not have and should not have been resolved through negotiations. In reality, it was power that was ultimately behind resolving every social and political conflict. In its extreme degree, this approach was implemented during the Stalin era, when everyone who did not share the official point of view was declared an "enemy of the people." Millions of people suffered from repressions and found themselves in prisons and concentration camps.

The next official position was that the Soviet society no longer had conflicts, since the socialist reconstruction had been completed and the ground for antagonistic contradictions had disappeared. It was believed that the root cause for internal conflicts had gone with the proletariat achieving "full and final victory in the USSR." Anything that did not fit this picture was classified and considered as atypical or abnormal. While describing internal affairs in the USSR, scholars even avoided the use of terminology of "conflict." In the field of ethnic studies, the notion of "new historic entity—the Soviet people" served the ideological purpose of demonstrating the absence of contradictions among different nationalities. Conflict was viewed as a symptom of bad management, and party officials of different levels did their best to conceal or at least play down conflictual situations. In other words, the post-war era was marked by ideologically sanctioned inaction in conflict situations. This is understandable from a psychological point of view, since it served to compensate for the total conflict that characterized Stalin's era, a period that cost the society millions of lives.

The situation was more complicated in the international sphere. Interest in studying negotiation fluctuated, depending on relations with the West. That interest rose with improvement of Soviet-West relations and declined with this relationship's stalemates. Some obvious failures of the strategy of applying force in order to achieve political results further increased interest to studying negotiations. In general, one could identify the following periods in the Soviet/ Russian research on negotiations:

- Emergence of the first interest in studying negotiations processes and the appearance of the first works on this subject in Russian (1940s— early 1970s).

- Beginning of the development of a national negotiations research agenda (mid-1970s—early 1980s).
- Flourishing of negotiations research (end of 1980s—first half of 1990s) in the USSR/Russia.
- Decline of interest to the negotiations *problematique* (second half of 1990s—early 2000s).

It is important to note that this periodization is tentative and defined primarily by the appearance of significant published works.

2. The Soviet experience in negotiations studies

Initially, historical studies dominated the research on negotiations. Historians provided empirical descriptions of various negotiations conducted by Tsarist Russia, the USSR, and other states. The first wave of research examined negotiations in the area of diplomacy and offered detailed studies of the very process of negotiations, along with positions taken by the parties, types of concessions, and negotiations' results. At this stage, negotiations began to be viewed as a fundamental method of conducting international affairs, and classical works by Nikolson (1941), Satow (1944), and Cambon (1946) were translated into Russian. Above all, the interest stemmed from the practical necessity to prepare a new diplomatic corps. As Troyanovski (1941, 16) wrote in the introduction to Nikolson's *Diplomacy*, "study of the history of diplomacy and knowledge of diplomatic practices and international relations are essential tasks for our diplomatic personnel."

At about the same time, there appeared new Soviet studies that focused on the conduct of multilateral negotiations as well as negotiations held in international organizations. Researchers' main focus was on procedural questions and on the rules of conducting negotiations and conferences. In this context it is worth mentioning the chapter by Konchalovski "Organizational forms, international legal fundamentals, and the technique of modern diplomacy," published in a three-volume history of diplomacy (Istoriya diplomatii 1945, 765-816), which became indispensable to many generations of Soviet diplomats. Along with issues of diplomatic immunity and diplomatic correspondence, the chapter detailed such issues as conference opening and language used by negotiations' participants. At the time, this was the accepted way of analyzing negotiations held in international organizations, particularly in the United Nations (Morozov 1962).

The first book-length studies of negotiations' conduct and mediation (Bogdanov 1957; Ladyzhenski and Blishchenko 1963; Pushmin 1970, 1974) appeared in the period between 1950s and early 1970s and were written in the international law tradition. Negotiations were finally becoming a direct object of scholarly interest, although procedural issues still dominated the research. For instance, experimental and mathematical methods of research so common in the West were practically non-existent in the Soviet Union.[1]

In the second half of the 1970s, interest to negotiations' *problematique* rose significantly, a development precipitated first and foremost by relaxation of the Soviet-West tensions. That interest was centered on critical foreign policy issues. Foreign Minister V. Petrovski and Deputy Foreign Minister A. Kovalev were instrumental in initiating the development of negotiations research. In his book *Azbuka Diplomatii* (ABC of Diplomacy), Kovalev (1977) was one of the first to introduce Western knowledge in the field to the Soviet readers. His volume sustained a number of editions and served as a key text for several generations of diplomats. The book emphasized the need for developing interdisciplinary and applied research on negotiations. Petrovski (1976) also offered analysis of Western approaches to international relations in general and negotiations in particular.

These developments stimulated research on negotiations, which concentrated, at the time, at the Moscow State Institute of International Relations (MGIMO) and the Academy of Diplomacy—academic institutions that were attached to the Soviet Ministry of Foreign Affairs and were responsible for educating diplomatic cadres. Diplomats continued to impact the scholarly community.[2] A bit later, institutions of the Soviet Academy of Sciences, such as the

---

[1] That was despite availability of a translation of Neiman's and Morgenstern's book "Game Theory and Economic Behavior" (1970).

[2] See, for example, the book by Dmitrichev (1981) on the process and practice of diplomatic negotiations.

Institute of the USA and Canada (ISKAN) and the Institute of Social Science Information (INION), also took interest in developing negotiations research (Peregovory 1981, 123-137).

MGIMO and its Problem Laboratory of Scientific Research, headed by I. Tyulin, played a special role in strengthening the trend of independent research on negotiations. Supported by Petrovski and Kovalev, the laboratory produced some unusually innovative research. In the Soviet era, it was one of the first to adopt modern methods of analysis so popular in the United States. At the same time, it was not too dependent on Western works and produced its own original research (Tyulin and Khrustalev 1981, 1982; Ashin and Tyulin 1982). For example, V. Lukov and V. Sergeyev (1981) developed a computer model estimating positions of countries participating in negotiations. They defined "position" as a system which elements were reflected in participants' goals and propositions and in their evaluations by other participants. The developed model was then tested by analyzing the Conference on the Security and Cooperation in Europe. It allowed tracing of the evolution of Conference participants' positions and to determine the areas of their compatibility and divergence. The model's success prompted some foreign scholars (Frei 1984) to refer to it as highly productive.

Another study developed by the "Problem Laboratory" had to do with analysis of negotiations' tactics. Its staff (Lebedeva 1981) defined the process of negotiations as composed of the means of presenting a position, the stages of negotiation conduct, and the various tactical methods employed by the negotiators. Kovaleva and Lebedeva (1981) then proposed to monitor the negotiation process along the identified dimensions. This line of research was once again praised highly by foreign experts.[3] At the same time, scholars at the Academy of Diplomacy attempted applying computer methodologies in researching negotiation processes. During this period, very few other Soviet authors were trying to use mathematical methods of analysis, modeling, and application of information technology in their research.

---

[3]   In particular, the American researcher P. Bennett (1997), while referring to the work of Zagorski and Lebedeva (1989) wrote that in research on tactiques of negotations, the Soviet researchers had been farther along than their American colleagues.

The period of 1970s and the early 1980s saw a continued interest of Soviet scholars in accomplishments of their foreign colleagues and the development of studies of conflicts and cooperation in relation to negotiations (Vneshnep-oliticheskie koflikty i mezhdunarodnye krizisy 1979; Voprosy teorii i praktiki dip-lomaticheskikh peregovorov 1981; Doronina 1981). In addition, scholars continued to be interested in historical-descriptive studies of negotiations (Beletski 1979). Scholarship, however, continued to be centered on the needs of negotiations' practitioners and did not affect academic programs and universities. There were no special courses on negotiations, even in specialized educational institutions responsible for educating diplomatic personnel. Diplomats were supposed to master the skills of negotiations on their own, an approach that echoed the accepted European approach to educating diplomats. As a result, despite some serious accomplishments, the field of negotiations in the Soviet Union remained highly "exotic" and remained a preserve of a very narrow circle of scholars. The contrast with negotiations research that was booming in the United States was especially striking.

A number of factors constrained further development of Soviet negotiation studies. Perhaps the most important one was that the Soviet Union was only interested in negotiations in the area of international relations, which severely limited social demand for negotiations research. Analytically, three disciplines dominated the field of international relations—history, law, and economics. Although attempts to apply other disciplines, such as sociology and psychology, to studying international processes and negotiations existed (Burlatski and Galkin 1974; Ermolenko 1977; Lebedeva 1981, 1982; Kosolapov 1983; Egorova 1988), they did not really spring roots. International studies were, therefore, of multidisciplinary, rather than interdisciplinary, nature.

The Marxist orientation dominant in Soviet social sciences was another factor impeding development of negotiations research. On the one hand, the Marxist-Leninist doctrine of class struggle in the international arena degraded negotiations to the status of temporary tactical maneuvers insignificant in the larger historical perspective. International partners could hardly appreciate such a view of negotiations. On the other hand, the official concept of peaceful coexistence of states belonging to different social formation made negotiations essential to resolving international disputes. It sent contradictory signals to both practitioners and scholars. Over time, the idea of class struggle lost its dominant status, surrendering to that of détente and interstate cooperation. Interest to the *problematique* of cooperation and negotiation was growing anew. This direction, although not smooth in its development, nevertheless prevailed.

3. The rise of a national research school on negotiations

The changes occurring in the Soviet Union between the late 1980s and the early 1990s had eliminated many of the constraints of the past, such as the Marxist dogmas and the lack of interest to Western scholarship in social science. In the late 1980s, Liberalism replaced Realism and pioneered the idea of universal human values. The new stage of openness and détente in the international arena provided a new impetus to the development of negotiations studies. Another favorable context was provided by the expansion of entrepreneurship, which is unthinkable without negotiations. Finally, new conflicts, both social and ethnic, required search for peaceful ways to solve them. All these changes favored the development of negotiation studies, and comparative methods began to be employed by Russian scholars (Lebedeva 1994a, b).

Scholars of international relations were among the first to react to the new social demand for better understanding of negotiations between states. Specialized journals, such as *International Affairs*, *World Economy and International Relations*, *USA: Economics, Politics, and Ideology*, developed a strong interest in negotiation *problematique*. The progress was significant in part because negotiations scholarship was finally available to a larger audience outside of Moscow.

It is worth noting some special characteristics of this period. First, a purely scientific and heavily quantitative orientation that had come from the United States and had dominated the late 1970s and early 1980s, was now in decline. Qualitative research was back everywhere, including America. Interest in case studies was revived (Dmitrichev 1988). Secondly, more efforts were made to learn some practical lessons from negotiations of the past. Many practitioners acknowledged that international negotiations had become too complex and not as effective and that an effort had to be made to improve them. Third, negotiations began to be understood in a broader international context, a step which went beyond the overemphasis on technological aspects of negotiations and the strategies and tactics of negotiation conduct. Analysis of world development trends was now understood to be important for understanding the specifics of negotiations. In the new international context, diplomacy and negotiations were no longer viewed as a continuation of international conflict by political means. In V. Lukov's (1988, 118) words, negotiations were now "a means of conflict prevention" rather than conflict continuation.[4]

Kremenyuk (1988) addressed the latter development and suggested the emergence of an international negotiations system, a system which unified formal and informal procedures of conflict resolution and had become universal by the end of the 20th century. In his view, this system was based on rules of non-violence, cooperation, and collaborative search for a solution. The following were the characteristics of his proposed model:

- The new system of international negotiations increasingly reflected the existing structure of conflicts and disputes. It was more universal than ever before, and it combined formal and informal procedures of conflict resolution;

- Within a larger system of international relations, the negotiation system was becoming increasingly independent, with its own laws and rules of behavior;

- An increasingly universal system, the international negotiations system contributed to stabilization and development of the international system;

- Participants in contemporary negotiations were becoming more interested in going beyond their own self-interests and toward satisfying interests of their partners.

Interestingly enough, at about the same time some American authors began to call for a more orderly conduct of international negotiations in the

---

[4] Lukov (1998) also identified some new and negative aspects of the negotiation process often a result of the US behavior in the international arena. In particular, he wrote about slowing the negotiation processes and damaging the partner's reputation as means of strengthening a participant's position.

interests of avoiding redundancy and ineffectiveness. In particular, Fisher (Internatsionalizatsiya dialoga 1989) proposed the idea of a negotiations' hierarchy, where negotiations were ranked based on their significance—from unofficial exchanges of opinions among experts to the level of official negotiations. He also pointed to the possibility of international collaboration between experts in the development of decision-making models and emphasized the transition from confrontation to an analysis of collaborative problems.

From the late 1980s through the 1990s, it became a common practice in the USSR/Russia to invite foreign negotiation researchers to speak at scientific seminars and conferences and to visit research centers. Leading scholars of negotiations actively published their work in Russian academic journals (Internatsionalizatsiya dialoga 1989; Iskusstvo diplomaticheskikh peregovorov 1989; Rubin and Kolb 1990; Rubin and Salakuze 1990), and many of their books (e.g. Mastenbrook 1993; Fisher and Ury 1990; Kornelius and Feyr 1992; Koren and Goodmen 1995; Broyning 1996; Fisher and Ertel 1996; Nirenberg 1996; Karras 1997) were translated into Russian. The presence of American scholars was particularly visible. The book by Fisher and Ury (1990) was especially popular. One should note that translations into Russian were not limited to Moscow but also took place in other cities of Russia and the former Soviet republics. In their turn, Russian scholars worked hand in hand with their foreign colleagues in keeping up with principal developments in the negotiation field (Kokoshin, Kremenyuk, and Sergeyev 1989) and actively participating in various international projects.[5]

In terms of empirical emphasis, the issues of Soviet-American negotiations remained the center of attention (e.g. Kremenyuk 1990, 1991a, b). However, theoretical knowledge began to grow in importance. The development of new information and communication technologies further aided the emergence of new dimensions in the theory and practice of negotiations (Potter 1990; Pryakhin 1987).

The last two important features of this period were the emergence of textbooks on negotiations (Zagorski and Lebedeva 1989; Israelyan 1990; Lebedeva 1993) and the expansion of negotiation research beyond international

---

[5] The collective volume edited by V. Kremenyuk (1991) became especially widely cited.

relations. Russian textbooks on negotiations, along with the introduction of courses on negotiation in academic curricula, gave the negotiation discipline the long sought academic status. A course on negotiations soon became mandatory in university curricula on international relations. In addition, economists developed interest to studying negotiation (Ernst 1988; Kornelius and Feyer 1992; Mastenbrook 1993). There was also an effort to systematize the acquired knowledge on negotiations for practitioners (Israelyan and Lebedeva 1991).

4. The post-Soviet paradox: vanishing negotiations *problematique* vs. the demand for research

Negotiation studies in Russia seemed to have gained momentum, and one might have expected a further boom of research in the area, similar to what was happening in the United States. Instead, the mid-1990s witnessed an obvious decline of the field. There were both external and internal explanations for the decline.

Externally, the overall number of publications on negotiations somewhat declined. Following the dissolution of the USSR and the Warsaw Pact, the negotiation in the area of arms control lost their former urgency. At the same time, new conflicts emerged in the world, including conflicts in Europe. These two factors shifted researchers' attention away from the issues of conducting negotiations and towards questions related to conflict prevention and resolution. Many of those who had earlier studied negotiations' strategies now moved to the area of conflicts. Various branches of the Academy of Sciences, as well as other scientific and educational centers in Russia, concentrated their efforts on conflict resolution.

Another reason for the shift towards conflict study had to do with the changing nature of the world's conflicts. Increasingly, conflicts became internal (Wallensteen and Sollenberg 1995; Lebedeva 1998), and some new non-state actors, like ethnic groups, became active participants in them. The other participants, states and international organizations, now had to negotiate with minority groups who strive for autonomy within the existing system. The old models of complex negotiations, developed earlier specifically for interstate communication, now seemed applicable for confronting new challenges in the new environment.

These external tendencies influenced Russian negotiation research. In the mid-1990s, negotiations were increasingly viewed as an internal tool (Lebedeva 1993b, 1994a, b), and interest in conflicts began to dominate the agenda of scholars. The culturally specific feature of Russian studies was that they tried to understand the underlying origins and causes of conflicts (Nasinovski and Skakunov 1995; Rainer 1995; Feldman 1997, 1998; Olkott, Tishkov, and Malashenko 1997; Popov 1997; Arutyunyan, Drobizheva, and Susokova 1998; Payin 1998; Zerkin 1998) rather than the process of conflict resolution.[6] Special attention was given to ethnic conflicts and their roots—hardly a surprise when one considers the primacy and significance of these conflicts to Russia. An explanation for such focus on the causes and stages of conflict development rather than on conflict resolution can be found in Russian scientific tradition. Whereas in America a strong emphasis is put upon pragmatism, and scholarly attention is typically devoted to the techniques of negotiation conduct, in Europe and Russia, the focus is on underlying and originating factors. As the joke goes, Russians like to ask the "Who is guilty?" rather than "What should one do?"

In addition, many of the conflicts that took place in Russia and other states of the former USSR were hard to solve through negotiation processes. Typically, conflict situations either escalated into open military resistances, as in Chechnya in 1994 or Moscow in 1993, or—due to external peacekeeping interventions—turned into "cold peace" situations, as in Abkhazia and Moldova. Cases of reaching agreements through negotiations were rather rare (Lebedeva 2000). The best example might be Tatarstan in 1994, when conflict with Moscow was resolved peacefully, to a great extend because of the personal efforts of the President of Tatarstan M. Shaimiyev.

The low emphasis on negotiations as a conflict resolution strategy was, to a significant degree, the result of a weak negotiation culture, which took

---

[6] Exceptions included some works on conflict resolution (Lebedeva 1997), legal aspects of conflicts (Kudryavtsev 1995), and peacekeeping (Nikitin, Khlestov, Fedorov, and Demurenko 1998).

decades and even centuries to develop. For many years, the USSR had developed the experience only of international negotiations. Experience of internal conflict resolution through negotiations was absent. The result was a widely spread skepticism regarding negotiations, and a decline of research on negotiations as a conflict resolution strategy.

The final reason for why negotiation studies failed to progress in post-Soviet Russia was lack of financial support. In the 1990s, Russia was too pre-occupied with its economic and internal political problems, and the state funding for research was cut abruptly. Under such conditions, negotiations, as well as other fields of research, were simply not viewed as a priority neither by the state nor by the mass media.

5. The future of negotiations studies

What are the prospects of negotiation studies in the world in general and in Russia in particular? To answer this question, one must take into consideration international tendencies in the development of the field, as well as Russia's own scientific processes and capabilities.

In the early 21st century, negotiations continue to be at the center of scholarly attention, especially in the United States. Following a wave of interest in conflict resolution in the mid-1990s, negotiation research agenda seems to be coming back. The field is also developing some new areas of research, such as negotiation types, cultural styles of negotiations, unofficial mediation, interactions of non-state actors with state representatives, relations between legal procedures, negotiation strategies in conflict resolution, and so on.

Meanwhile, in Russia, negotiations and skills of their conduct seem to be of prime interest to business schools. Presently, there are a number of programs offering courses on negotiations. Their academic level, however, leaves much to be desired and often does not meet even minimal standards. Books of Russian and foreign authors offering recommendations regarding negotiation conduct (Donaldson and Donaldson 2000; Bellanzhe 2002; Mokshantsev 2002; Shatin 2002; Mitroshenkov 2003) continue to appear. But most of them do not go beyond recommendations that are based on common sense and knowledge of some general psychology. They do not even attempt to venture into comparative studies in order to develop some theoretical generalizations, a practice that is prevalent in the West. Only a few Russian researchers, such as Kremenyuk, continue to publish abroad (Kremenyuk and Sjostedt 2000).

Occasionally, interesting works do appear. And although they are few in number, they do succeed in originating different trends. Among them, one might mention the book by V. Sergeyev *Democracy as a Negotiation Process*, in which the author makes a distinction between two types of social organization and management—hierarchical and democratic. The former assumes the society's surrendering to the authority, whereas the latter means a constant search for social consensus through negotiations. The author maintains that democracy is impossible without negotiation processes, and in this respect, democracy equals negotiations. The approach might open up some new opportunities for negotiation studies, as well as for analysis of democracy and democratization. Global democratization processes can then be analyzed from the logical standpoint of negotiation studies.

Generally speaking, one would expect that the most productive areas of negotiation research will be focused on the broader contexts of international political processes. One might notice a certain paradox: past systems of international relations, such as the Versailles or Yalta-Potsdam system, were established as a result of post-war negotiations, a context which was conspicuously missing at the end of the Cold War. Why negotiations did not play their traditional role here remains to be researched. It is clear, however, that the changes in the contemporary world run deep, and they are not only limited to changes in interstate relations. Rather, the world is in process of departure from Westphalia system toward something new and yet unknown. It also seems clear that future negotiation studies will have to integrate a variety of other issues, such as political decision-making, political management, interactions between state and non-state actors, global management, and others. The rise of terrorism also raises the question of the limits of negotiations. It urges us to ask again if one can, in fact, negotiate with terrorists, drug-traffickers, and highly corrupt and totalitarian regimes.

One can also expect continued research interest into multilateral negotiations, as well as into negotiations conducted on different levels, with the participation of both state and non-state actors, namely Trans-National Corporations and political and social movements. The complexity of the negotiation process is likely to increase in terms of negotiations' content, procedures, and processes. This will call for new analytical approaches. The expansion of negotiation participants makes it urgent and necessary to educate the public about the various aspects of negotiation processes and the interactions between professional and non-professional participants. There is also a need to increase the number of analyzed cases to include those in commercial, ecological, and other areas, thus improving our understanding of negotiations' successes and failures.

These are only some possible directions for further research on negotiation. Unfortunately, Russia has stayed away from pursuing either one of the outlined directions. Foreign scholars are more active than the Russian ones, even when it comes to the study of the Russian negotiation style, despite the obvious advantage this subject has for Russian researchers. Will the status of Russian negotiation studies change? Some grounds for hope do exist. Russia has always had high creative potential. It has also taken the loss of its former international status close to heart and became very interested in active participation in the newly emerging world order. In this world, harmonization of interests through negotiations of new mutually acceptable rules will be a main principle.

References

Arutyunyan, Y. V. , L. M. Drobizheva, A. A. Susokolov. 1998. Etnosotsiologiya. Aspekt-Press, Moskva.

Atkinson, G. 1980. The Effective Negotiator. Quest, Leningrad.

Ashyn, G. K., I. G. Tyulin, eds. 1982. V. I. Lenin i dialektika sovremennykh mezhdunarodnykh otnosheniy. MGIMO, Moskva.

Bellanzhe, L. 2002. Peregovory. Neva, St. Perersburg.

Beletskiy, V. N. 1979. Za stolom peregovorov. Politizdat, Moskva.

Bennet, P. R. 1997. Russian Negotiating Strategy. Nova Science Publishers, New York.

Bogdanov, O. V. 1957. Peregovory—osnovnoe sredstvo uregoulirovaniya mezhdunarodnykh raznoglasiy. Sovetskoye gosoudarstvo i pravo 7.

Broyning, G. 1996. Rukovodstvo po vedeniyu peregovorov. INFRA-M, Moskva.

Burlatski, F. M., A. A. Galkin. 1974. Sotsiologiya. Politika. Mezhdunarodnye otnosheniya. Mezhdunarodnye otnosheniya, Moskva.

Dmitrichev, T. F. 1981. Mnogostoronnaya diplomatiya Soedinennykh Shtatov Ameriki. Mezhdunarodnye otnosheniya, Moskva.

Dmitrichev, T. F. 1988. Zhenevskie foroumy peregovorov po razoruzheniyu 1945-1987. Mezhdunarodnye otnosheniya, Moskva.

Donaldson, M. 2000. Umenie vesti peregovory. Dialektika, Moskva.

Doronina, N. I. 1981. Mezhdunarodnyi konflikt. Mezhdunarodnye otnosheniya, Moskva.

Egorova, E. V. 1988. Soedinennye Shtaty Ameriki v mezhdunarodnykh krizisakh. Nauka, Moskva.

Ermolenko, D. V. 1977. Sotsiologiya i problemy mezhdunarodnykh otnosheniy. Mezhdunarodnye otnosheniya, Moskva.

Ernst, O. 1988. Slovo predostavleno vam. Ekonomika, Moskva.

Feldman, D. M. 1997. Konflikty v mirovoi politike. "Bratya Karich," Moskva.

Feldman, D. M. 1998. Politologiya konflikta. Strategiya, Moskva.

Fisher, R. and W. Ury. 1990. Getting to Yes. Nauka, Moskva.

Fisher, R. and D. Ertel. 1996. Podgotovka k peregovoram. Filin', Moskva.

Frei, D., ed. 1984. Assumptions and Perceptions in Disarmament. United Nations Publication, New York.

Held, D. 1989. Political Theory and the Modern State. Stanford University Press, Stanford.

Hirschson, J. 1996. Negotiating a Democratic Order in South Africa. Negotiation Journal 12 (2).

Internatsionalizatsiya dialoga i peregovornykh protsessov. Discussion. 1989. Mezhdunarodnaya zhizn' 1.

Iskusstvo diplomaticheskikh peregovorov. 1989. Mezhdunarodnaya zhizn', 8.

Israelyan, V. L. 1990. Diplomaty litsom k litsu. Mezhdunarodnye otnosheniya, Moskva.

Israelyan, V. and M. Lebedeva. 1991. Peregovory—iskusstvo dlia vsekh. Mezhdunarodnaya zhizn' 11.

Istoriya diplomatii. 1945. Izdatel'stvo politicheskoi literatury, Moskva-Leningrad.

Kambon, J. 1945. Diplomat. Gospolitizdat, Moskva-Leningrad.

Karras, Ch. 1997. Iskusstvo vedeniya peregovorov. EKSMO, Moskva.

Kokoshin, A. A., V. A. Kremenyuk, V. M. Sergeyev. 1989. Voprosy
issledovaniya mezhdunarodnykh peregovorov. Mirovaya ekonomika i
mezhdunarodnye otnosheniya 9.

Koppiters, B., E. Remakl, A. Zverev. 1997. Mezhdunarodny opyt razresheniya
etnicheskikh konfliktov. Karnegi, Moskva.

Koren, L. and P. Goodmen. 1995. Iskusstvo torgovatsya, ili vse o
peregovorakh. Rodny Kout, Minsk.

Kornelius, H. and Sh. Feyr. 1992. Vyigrat' mozhet kazhdyi. Stringer, Moskva.

Kosolapov, N. A. 1983. Sotsialnaya psikhologuiya i mezhdunarodnye
otnosheniya. Nauka, Moskva.

Kovalev, A. G. 1977. Azbuka diplomatii. Mezhdunarodnye otnosheniya,
Moskva.

Kovaleva, O. M. and M. M. Lebedeva. 1981. Metodiki otsenki pozitsiy
uchastnikov mezhdunarodnykh peregovorov na osnove analiza vystupleniy.
In: Voprosy modelirovaniya mnogostoronnykh diplomaticheskikh
peregovorov. MGIMO, Moskva.

Kremenyuk, V. A. 1988. Formirovanie systemy mezhdunarodnogo
obshcheniya. In: Diplomaticheskiy vestnik, ed. by O.G. Peresypkin.
Mezhdunarodnye otnosheniya, Moskva.

Kremenyuk, V. A. 1990. Na puti uregulirovaniya konfliktov. Soedinennye
Shtaty Ameriki: ekonomika, politika, ideologiya 12.

Kremenyuk, V. A., ed. 1991. International Negotiations. Jossey-Bass, San
Francisco.

Kremenyuk, V. A. 1991. Problemy peregovorov v otnosheniyakh dvukh
derzhav. Soedinennye Shtaty Ameriki: ekonomika, politika, ideologiya 3.

Kudryavtsev, V. N., ed. 1995. Yuridicheskaya konfliktologiya. Institut
gosudarstva i prava, Moskva.

Ladyzhenskiy, A. M. and I. P. Blishenko. 1963. Mirnye sredstva razresheniya
sporov mezhdu gosudarstvami. Gosyurizdat, Moskva.

Lebedeva, M. M. 1981. Psikhologicheskie aspekty taktiki vedeniya
diplomaticheskikh peregovorov. Voprosy modelirovaniya mnogostoronnikh

diplomaticheskikh peregovorov, ed. by I. G. Tyulin, M. A. Khrustalev.
MGIMO, Moskva.

Lebedeva, M. M. 1982. Sotsialno-psikhologicheskie metody issledovaniya
diplomaticheskikh peregovorov. In: V. I. Lenin i dialektika sovremennykh
mezhdunarodnykh otnosheniy, ed. by A. G. Ashin, I. G. Tyulin. MGIMO,
Moskva.

Lebedeva, M. M. 1993. Vam predstoyat peregovory. Ekonomika, Moskva.

Lebedeva, M. M. 1993. Konflikty vnutri i vokrug Rossii: primenyat silu ili vesti
peregovory? MGIMO, Moskva.

Lebedeva, M.M. 1994. Samoopredeleniye regionov. Mezhdunarodnaya zhizn'
11.

Lebedeva, M. M. 1994. Conflict Management in Changing Society. In:
Multicultural Conflict Management in Changing Societies, ed. by Louise
Niewmeijer and Renee du Toit. HSRC, Pretoria.

Lebedeva, M. M. 1997. Politicheskoe uregulirovanie konfliktov. Aspekt-Press,
Moskva.

Lebedeva, M. M. 1998. Mezhdunarodnye protsessy. In: Mezhdunarodnye
otnosheniya, sotsiologicheskie podkhody, ed. by P. A. Tsygankov.
Gardarika, Moskva.

Lebedeva, M. M. 2000. Mezhetnicheskie konflikty na rubezhe vekov. Mirovaya
ekonomika i mezhdunarodnye otnosheniya 5.

Lukov, V. B. 1988. Sovremennye diplomaticheskie peregovory. In:
Diplomaticheski vestnik 1987, ed. by O.G. Peresypkin. Mezhdunarodnye
otnosheniya, Moskva.

Lukov, V. B. and V. M. Sergeyev. 1981. Metodologicheskie i metodicheskie
osnovy informatsionno-logicheskoi sistemy "SBSE." In: Voprosy
modelirovaniya mnogostoronnikh diplomaticheskikh peregovorov, edited by
I. G. Tyulin, M. A. Khrustalev. MGIMO, Moskva.

Mastenbrook, V. 1993. Peregovory. Kaluzhski institut sotsiologii, Kaluga.

Mokshantsev, R. I. 2002. Psikhologiya peregovorov. Infra-M, Moskva.

Morozov, G. I. 1962. Organizatsiya Obyedinennykh Natsiy. Mezhdunarodnye
otnosheniya, Moskva.

Nasinovskiy, V. V. and Z. I. Skakunov.1995. Politicheskie konflikty v sovremenykh usloviyakh. Soedinennye Shtaty Ameriki: ekonomika, politika, ideologiya 4.

Neiman, J. and O. Morgenstern. 1970. Game Theory and Economic Behavior. Nauka, Moskva.

Nikitin, A. I., O. N. Khlestov, E. Y. Fedorov, A. V. Demurenko. 1998. Mirotvorcheskie operatsii v SNG. MONF, Moskva.

Nikolson, G. 1941. Diplomatiya. OGIZ, Moskva.

Nirenberg, G. 1996. Maestro peregovorov. Paradox, Minsk.

Olkott, M. B., V. Tishkov, and A. Malashenko, eds. 1997. Identichnost' i konflikt. Moskovski Tsentr Karnegi, Moskva.

Pain, E. 1998. Chechnya i drugiye konflikty v Rossiyi. Mezhdunarodnaya zhizn' 9.

Petrovski, V. 1976. Amerikanskaya vneshnepoliticheskaya mysl'. Mezhdunarodnye otnosheniya, Moskva.

Pushmin, E. A. 1970. Posrednichestvo v mezhdunarodnom prave. Mezhdunarodnye otnosheniya, Moskva.

Pushmin, E. A. 1974. Mirnoye razresheniye mezhdunarodnykh sporov. Mezhdunarodnye otnosheniya, Moskva.

Popov, A. A. 1997. Prichiny vozniknoveniya i dialektika razvitiya mezhnatsionalnykh konfliktov. In: Identichnost' i konflikt v post-sovetskikh gosudarstvakh, edited by M. B. Olkott, V. Tishkov, and A. Malashenko. Moskovski Tsentr Karnegi, Moskva.

Potter, W. 1990. Modelirovanie Amerikano-Sovetskikh peregovorov po kontrolu nad vooruzheniyami. Soedinennye Shtaty Ameriki: ekonomika, politika, ideologiya 9.

Pryakhin, V. 1987. Novye sredstva v praktike diplomaticheskikh peregovorov. Mezhdunarodnaya zhizn 12.

Rainer, M. 1995. Teoriya konflikta. Polis 5.

Rubin, G., D. Kolb. 1990. Psikhologicheski podkhod k protsessam mezhdunarodnykh peregovorov. Psikhologicheski zhurnal 11 (2).

Rubin, G., G. Salakuze. 1990. Faktor sily v mezhdunarodnykh otnosheniyakh. Mezhdunarodnaya zhizn' 3.

Satow, E. 1944. Rukovodstvo po diplomaticheskoi praktike. OGIZ, Moskva.

Shatin, Y. V. 2002. Iskusstvo peregovorov. Berrator-Press, Moskva.

Troyanovski, A. A. 1941. Predislovie. G. Nikolson, "Diplomatiya." OGIZ, Moskva.

Tyulin, I. G. and M. A. Khrustalev, eds. 1981. Voprosy modelirovaniya mnogostoronnikh diplomaticheskikh peregovorov. MGIMO, Moskva.

Tyulin, I. G. and M. A. Khrustalev, eds. 1982. Analiticheskiye metody v issledovaniyi mezhdunarodnykh otnosheni. MGIMO, Moskva.

Vneshnepoliticheskiye koflikty i mezhdunarodnye krizisy. 1979. INION AN SSSR, Moskva.

Voprosy teoriyi i praktiki diplomaticheskikh peregovorov. 1981. INION AN SSSR, Moskva.

Wallensteen, P., M. Sollenberg. 1995. After the Cold War: Emerging Patterns of Armed Conflict, 1989-1994. Journal of Conflict Resolution 32.

Zagorski, A. V. and M. M. Lebedeva. 1988. Teoriya i metodologiya vedeniya mezhdunarodnykh peregovorov. MGIMO, Moskva.

Zerkin, D. P. 1998. Osnovy konfliktologii. Feniks, Rostov-na-Donu.

Authors

Alexei D. Bogaturov
Director, Moscow Educational Forum on International Relations. Editor-in-chief of "International Trends "(Mezhdunarodnie Protsessy).

Michail V. Il'yin
Professor, Department of Political Science, Moscow Institute of International Relations. Editor-in-chief of "Political Studies" (Polis).

Marina V. Lebedeva
Professor, World Politics Chair, Moscow Institute of International Relations.

Nayil' M. Mukharyamov
Associate Professor, Department of Political Science, Kazan' State University.

Alexandr A. Sergunin
Professor, Department of International Relations and Political Science, Nizhni Novgorod Linguistic University.

Tatyana A. Shakleyina
Senior Reseacher, Institute of the USA and Canada Studies, Moscow.

Eduard G. Solovyev
Senior Reseacher, Institute of the World Economy and International Relations, Moscow.

Stanislav L. Tkachenko
Vice-Rector in International Relations, St. Petersburg State University.

Andrei P. Tsygankov
Assistant Professor, Departments of International Relations and Political Science, San Francisco State University. Email: andrei@sfsu.edu

Pavel A. Tsygankov
Professor, Sociology of International Relations Chair, Moscow State University. Email: tsygankp@redline.ru

Dr. Andreas Umland (Ed.)

SOVIET AND POST-SOVIET
POLITICS AND SOCIETY

ISSN 1614-3515

This book series makes available, to the academic community and general public, affordable English-, German- and Russian-language scholarly studies of various *empirical* aspects of the recent history and current affairs of the former Soviet bloc. The series features narrowly focused research on a variety of phenomena in Central and Eastern Europe as well as Central Asia and the Caucasus. It highlights, in particular, so far understudied aspects of late Tsarist, Soviet, and post-Soviet political, social, economic and cultural history from 1905 until today. Topics covered within this focus are, among others, political extremism, the history of ideas, religious affairs, higher education, and human rights protection. In addition, the series covers selected aspects of major issues in post-Soviet transitions such as economic crisis, foreign policy, and constitutional reform.

SOVIET AND POST-SOVIET POLITICS AND SOCIETY

Edited by Dr. Andreas Umland

ISSN 1614-3515

Annette Freyberg-Inan
The Social Sciences in Romania
Research Conditions and the Role of International Support
ISBN 3-89821-416-8

Laura Victoir
The Russian Land Estate Today
ISBN 3-89821-426-5

Stephanie Solowyda
Biography of Semen Frank
ISBN 3-89821-457-5

Margaret Dikovitskaya
Arguing with the Photographs
Russian Imperial Colonial Attitudes in Visual Culture
ISBN 3-89821-462-1

Stefan Ihrig
Welche Nation in welcher Geschichte?
Eigen- und Fremdbilder der nationalen Diskurse in der Historiographie und den Geschichtsbüchern in der Republik Moldova, 1991-2003
ISBN 3-89821-466-4

David Galbreath
Nation-Building and Minority Politics
Interests, Influence and Identities
ISBN 3-89821-467-2

Christian Autengruber
Die politischen Parteien in Bulgarien und Rumänien
Eine vergleichende Analyse seit Beginn der 90er Jahre
ISBN 3-89821-476-1

Anastasiia Mitrofanova
The Politicization of Russian Orthodoxy
Actors and Ideas
ISBN 3-89821-481-8

Series Subscription

Hereby, I subscribe to the paperback book series **Soviet and Post-Soviet Politics and Society (ISSN 1614-3515)**

( ) starting with volume ____ **(number), or**

( ) starting with the next new volume.

In addition I am ordering herewith

( ) all previously published series volumes, or

( ) the following previously published book/s only:_____ (volume number/s).

The books should be sent to the address:

first, last name: _____

street: _____

*ZIP Code, city, country:*_____

*Tel.:*_____

date, signature: _____

Please fax to: **0511 / 262 2201 (+49 511 262 2201)**
or mail to: *ibidem*-Verlag, Julius-Leber-Weg 11, D-30457
Hannover,Germany
or send an e-mail: ibidem@ibidem-verlag.de

ibidem-Verlag

Melchiorstr. 15

D-70439 Stuttgart

info@ibidem-verlag.de

www.ibidem-verlag.de
www.edition-noema.de
www.autorenbetreuung.de